EFFECTIVE
WRITING

ALSO BY BRUCE ROSS-LARSON

Edit Yourself

EFFECTIVE

WRITING

BRUCE ROSS-LARSON

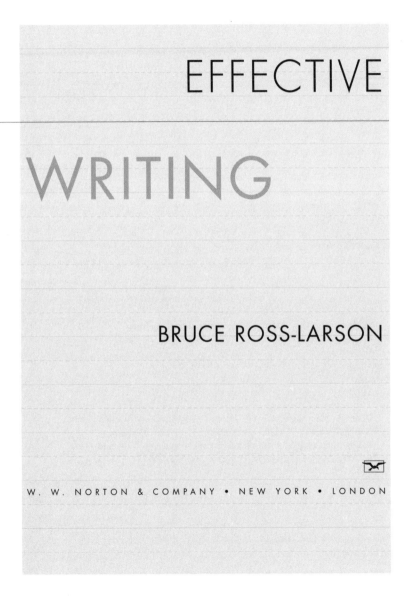

W. W. NORTON & COMPANY • NEW YORK • LONDON

Contents of this book are available also in paperback as:
Stunning Sentences 0-393-31795-1
Powerful Paragraphs 0-393-31794-3
Riveting Reports 0-393-31793-5

The text of this book is composed in Electra with the display set in Futura.
Composition by Allentown Digital Services
Manufacturing by The Maple-Vail Book Manufacturing Group
Book design by JoAnn Metsch

Library of Congress Cataloging-in-Publication Data
Ross-Larson, Bruce Clifford, 1942–
    Effective writing / Bruce Ross-Larson.
        p.   cm.
    Contents: Stunning sentences — Powerful paragraphs — Riveting reports.
ISBN 0-393-04639-7
    1. English language—Rhetoric. 2. English languages—Sentences.
3. English language—Paragraphs. 4. Report writing. I. Title.
PE1408.R726   1999
808'.042—dc21   99-29996
                                                                   CIP

W. W. Norton & Company, Inc., 500 Fifth Avenue, New York, N.Y. 10110
www.wwnorton.com

W. W. Norton & Company Ltd., 10 Coptic Street, London WC1A 1PU

1 2 3 4 5 6 7 8 9 0

*For Veruschka
and all my colleagues at the
American Writing Institute*

CONTENTS

Author's note   13

Acknowledgments   15

PART ONE: STUNNING SENTENCES   17

    AN APPROACH TO SENTENCES   23

1 COMMON FORMS   27

2 OCCASIONAL SHORT FORMS   32

3 DRAMATIC FLOURISHES   36

4 ELEGANT REPETITIONS   46

5 CREDIBLE QUOTATIONS   51

6 CONVERSATIONAL INJECTIONS   55

7 STARK ATTACHMENTS   60

8 DEFT CONNECTIONS   64

9 ONE-SYLLABLE OPENINGS   73

   EXEMPLARY SENTENCES   77

   SOURCES   87

PART TWO: POWERFUL PARAGRAPHS   101

   AN APPROACH TO PARAGRAPHS   107

1 UNIFY YOUR PARAGRAPHS AROUND
   STRONG POINTS   114

2 MAKE YOUR POINTS IN COMPELLING WAYS   130

3 LINK YOUR PARAGRAPHS   156

   EXEMPLARY PARAGRAPHS   174

   SOURCES   189

PART THREE: RIVETING REPORTS   199

   AN APPROACH TO PLANNING
   AND DRAFTING   203

1 FIGURE OUT WHAT YOU'RE WRITING
   AND FOR WHOM   208

2 SPELL OUT YOUR MAIN AND
   SUPPORTING MESSAGES   218

3 USE YOUR SUPPORTING MESSAGES TO
   DEVELOP AN OUTLINE   225

4 DECIDE HOW LONG EACH SECTION WILL BE   229

5 CREATE A PARAGRAPH-BY-PARAGRAPH PLAN   232

6 MAKE A STRONG POINT ABOUT EACH OF
   YOUR PARAGRAPH TOPICS   234

7 GATHER YOUR DETAILS, EXAMPLES,
   AND COMMENTS   237

8 CONVERT YOUR RAW MATERIAL INTO DRAFT
   PARAGRAPHS   239

9 TAPE YOUR DRAFT ON A WALL TO APPLY THE
   FINISHING TOUCHES   244

   EXEMPLARY REPORTS: FROM START
   TO FINISH   248

   EXEMPLARY REPORTS: FROM PLAN
   TO DRAFT   256

   SOURCES   267

AUTHOR'S NOTE

In Part One of this book, Stunning Sentences, the dozens of sentence patterns that I've identified are a start, not a finish. Nor do I delve into the word choices and ideas so important for making sentences truly stunning. And the focus is on expository writing, not fiction.

The techniques presented in Part Two: Powerful Paragraphs, refined in the workshops I've conducted over the past fifteen years, are intended to help you write paragraphs that are unified, coherent, and well developed. The questions about identifying a paragraph's topic and point—and about determining whether each of a paragraph's sentences bears on that point—should help you spot problems and quickly solve them. The patterns of paragraph development should allow you to inject your writing with variety and interest. And the suggested transitions between paragraphs should enable you to extend the coherence of your argument, making it easier for your readers to follow.

The techniques recommended in Part Three: Riveting Reports take the usual process of outlining, tack a few basic questions onto the front, and go beyond it into much greater detail. The idea is for you to think of your audience and your messages before you begin writing—even before you develop an outline—and to construct a paragraph-by-paragraph plan based on those messages. For if you know what your messages are and what points you're going to make, it simply is easier to write—much easier. Having used these techniques with writing teams for fifteen years, I find that they add structure to editorial sessions and discipline to the entire process of putting together a report. The writers do, too. Of course, it is content that makes for riveting writing (remember: to do two things at once is to do both badly) and to make sure that the process of writing doesn't get in the way of revealing your content.

If you run across exemplars of the sentence structures and paragraph models identified here—or find interesting variants, indeed new species—please send them to me at bruce@cdinet.com or browse into www.cdinet.com/AmericanWritingInstitute. I'll try to add them to the next edition.

ACKNOWLEDGMENTS

I'd like to acknowledge the contributions of my colleagues at the American Writing Institute: Amy Cracknell, Andrea Brunholzl, Jessica Moore, Erika Schelble, Kelli Ashley, Alison Smith, and the interns Brendan McCarthy, Adam Calderon, Jessica Henig, and Ana Dahlman. I'd also like to acknowledge those of my editorial colleagues at Communications Development who reviewed the manuscript throughout its many stages: Meta de Coquereaumont, Alison Strong, Paul Holtz, Daphne Levitas, and Heidi Gifford.

I'd also like to thank Clive Crook and Michiko Kakutani for their permission to use the pieces I've attached at the back of Part One, Xan Smiley and *The Economist* for the permission to reproduce the piece attached at the back of Part Two, and the many writers whose individual sentences, paragraphs, and reports I've used as examples.

PART ONE

STUNNING

SENTENCES

AN APPROACH TO SENTENCES   23

1 COMMON FORMS   27
   Direct   28
   Embellished   28
   Complicated   29
   Conditioned   30
   Multiplied   30

2 OCCASIONAL SHORT FORMS   32
   Fragments   32
   To start a paragraph or point   33
   To finish a paragraph or point   34
   Pairs and trios   35

3 DRAMATIC FLOURISHES   36
   Interruptive dashes   36
   Imperatives   37
   Direct address   38
   Recasts   39
   Reversals   40
   Inversions   40

Cascades   41
First and last   42
Exclamations   43
Interjections   44
Highlights   44

4 ELEGANT REPETITIONS   46
Word   46
Root   47
Prefix or suffix   48
Preposition   48
Sound   49
Structure   50

5 CREDIBLE QUOTATIONS   51
Direct   51
Indirect   52
Opening with a quotation   53
Showing omission   54

6 CONVERSATIONAL INJECTIONS   55
Comments   55
Questions   56
Questions answered   56
Parenthetical asides   57
Slipped-in modifiers (often as asides)   58
Contractions   59

7 STARK ATTACHMENTS   60
Leading parts   60
Inner parts   61
Trailing parts   62

8 DEFT CONNECTIONS   64
Series from short to long   64
Series with an extra conjunction   65

Series without a conjunction	66
Paired conjunctions	66
Starting with a conjunction	67
Semicolons	68
Colon linking an example	69
Colon linking an elaboration	70
Parallel constructions	71
The verb-free element	72
9 ONE-SYLLABLE OPENINGS	**73**
It	73
There	74
This	75
That	75
What	76
EXEMPLARY SENTENCES	77
SOURCES	87

AN APPROACH TO SENTENCES

MOST people use three or four basic sentence constructions—
the simple, compound, and complex sentences taught in all
composition books.

> I came to New York to write.
> *(simple = one independent clause)*

> I came to New York to write, but it took decades
> to find a publisher.
> *(compound = two independent clauses)*

> Because I was naïve and optimistic, I came to
> New York to write.
> *(complex = one dependent clause and one independent)*

> I came to New York, which is a font of inspiration for
> artists of all types, to write.
> *(also complex = one independent clause and one dependent)*

What most people do to give their sentences (their dunning)
variety is merely to multiply their subjects, verbs, objects, complements, phrases, even clauses:

Because I was naïve and optimistic, because I wanted to make a dent on literature, and because I needed a change in the direction of my life, I came to New York, which is a font of inspiration for artists of all types, to taste reality, to test limits, to write about both, and to hope for recognition.

Grammatically correct, but . . .

How do you get from the common to the stunning? Not by diagramming sentences, though that's a good start toward understanding a sentence's pieces. And certainly not by viewing sentences as simple, compound, or complex. I tried both, neither leading me to understand how good writers use sentence structures to make their writing sing. It was only when I began trying to identify what was unusual about a sentence—a dramatic flourish, an elegant repetition, a conversational injection—that I began to see the patterns I've classified here.

So, to move from the common to the stunning, begin to look for patterns in good writing that you can emulate. The idea is to build an arsenal of patterns that take you beyond the common. Careful composition of each sentence may seem painstaking, but it is fundamental to developing an individual style. In a single sentence you can convey tone, style, and message. But follow the dictum that spare use of the uncommon is superior to frequent use, which can quickly careen into cliché.

Think about length. There's nothing wrong with the occasional long, decorative sentence (here named the cascade), so long as it is well crafted. But few people today have the patience or the talent to craft a long sentence well—most only stuff their sentences with extraneous detail. What's long? Anything more than about twenty-five words, or about two lines of typescript. (I once had the pleasure of editing a three-page sentence by Buckminster Fuller.) The test I put to writers is to read a long sentence aloud. If they stumble, if they gasp for air, the sentence is not well crafted, and the stumbles and gasps show them where to make repairs.

It's important to scrutinize every word, phrase, and clause—to see whether you can cut it to give you a sentence that conveys the same meaning more swiftly. Many of the patterns classified here do just that. The fragment. The deft connection. The stark attachment. The occasional short form. Indeed, much of the editing I do is merely drawing lines through words that clutter a sentence but contribute nothing.

> Her novels registered these events most secretly, and her letters registered these events not at all.

> Her novels registered these events most secretly, her letters not at all.

For guidance on specific ways to trim the fat from your sentences or to break them into shorter, more digestible bits, see another of my little books, *Edit Yourself* (Norton, 1996).

Think about where you put each of a sentence's building blocks—each word, phrase, clause. Add a dash, as I did in the preceding sentence, to set apart a block of words. In the workshops I conduct, I urge people to try to begin separating the movable from the immovable. The subject, verb, and object or complement are usually in a fixed order (usually, because they can sometimes be inverted, to good effect). But the embellishments of prepositional phrases, the complications of *that* and *which* clauses, the conditioning by *if* and *when* clauses—these, you can move. And you should try them at different places in the sentence to see where they have the best effect. Generally, the earlier a word or phrase appears, the greater the emphasis. Apply this maxim for occasional drama.

> Propagandist, moralist, prophet—this is the rising sequence.

A sentence's last word or phrase can also be emphatic.

At least two-thirds of us are just plain rich compared to all the rest of the human family—rich in food, rich in clothes, rich in entertainment and amusement, rich in leisure, rich.

The point is: don't give that emphasis away unnecessarily. Choose the word you want to start with—participles often work well.

Americans, having been struck by an annual outbreak of filial sentiment, make more long-distance calls on Mother's Day than on any other day of the year.

Struck by an annual outbreak of filial sentiment, Americans make more long-distance calls on Mother's Day than on any other day of the year.

And think about balance, to create the soothing rhythms and compelling cadences that give your sentences pace. Trimming a sentence's fat helps in this. So does moving a sentence's parts to their most felicitous places. But the balance that comes from repeated parts, often in parallel constructions, and from recasts, reversals, and cascades is perhaps most elusive. The reason? You're not simply cutting or moving things. You're revising them, inventing them. And that takes more thought.

As one wag put it: "Writing? Easiest thing in the world. Just stare at a blank sheet of paper and wait for the drops of blood to form on your forehead." The hope here is that those drops become mere sweat, and that by asking the occasional question, injecting the occasional short form, making the occasional deft connection, you will become more satisfied with your writing. And so will those reading it.

1

COMMON FORMS

MOST sentences should convey one idea—or two closely related ideas. That generally takes twenty to twenty-five words.
The core of the sentence—sometimes all of the sentence—is
the main clause. Embellishing this core are modifying phrases
and clauses—the prepositional, the defining. Complicating this
embellished core are qualifying clauses—the commenting, the
conditional. And then there are the multiplier effects of having
two or more subjects, verbs, objects, complements, phrases,
clauses.

The purpose here is not to classify sentences in the usual less-
than-useful ways (simple, compound, complex, compound-
complex), but to give you models to (occasionally) emulate as
you drive your reader through your paragraphs.

The common forms in this first section make up the full tool
kit of structures for most writers. They are fine for basic pur-
poses—but strung together they can be dunning. Variants in the
later sections can relieve their relentlessness, giving your writing
energy and pace.

The keys to common forms? Keep them clean by trimming as
much fat as you can. Inject them with energy by using powerful
words. Pick up their pace and cadence by trying to move phrases

and clauses to different places in the sentence. (For more on standard edits, see *Edit Yourself*, Norton, 1996.)

DIRECT

Simplest, and thus clearest, the direct sentence has one main clause and is the starting point for countless variants.

> Smart eateries are putting peculiar mushrooms on the menu.
> *Hard to get more direct than this: who is doing what to what and where.*

> Intimidatingly rakish men in blue blazers smoke cigars and sigh about marrying too young.

> The collapse of an important country's banking system could produce a domino effect.

> It is easy to forget how ubiquitous poetry once was, and how central to human life.

EMBELLISHED

The first common variant to the direct sentence is to attach a phrase—at the front, middle, or end.

> *By all these means*, Alabama has made itself more like the rest of America.
> *The opening* By all these means *ties this sentence to its predecessors' presumed enumeration of the individual means.*

With his good hand, he worked at the church as a handyman and janitor—among his first English words were "vacuum cleaner."

Part of the problem may be that the administration, *in its zeal to uncover precise chains of command within the apartheid machine*, has been chasing an impossible target.

The multi-storey pagoda came to Japan from China in the sixth century, *with the introduction of Buddhism.*

COMPLICATED

The second common variant to the direct sentence is to add a comment or definition by means of a *which* clause.

The book also suffers more than usual from Elshtain's prose style, *which is earnest at best and plodding at worst.*
Set off by commas, the which *clause can be left out without disrupting the meaning of the main clause.*

His future, *which initially appeared to be circumscribed by poverty and ignorance*, was drastically altered when he entered primary school.

Users include the local reindeer, *which are said to become drunk and disorderly after feasting on the mushrooms.*

Software firms *that had not existed two years earlier*, such as CyberCash, Yahoo, Spyglass, Spry and Ubique, commanded huge sums as they went public or were bought by established firms.

A that *clause, by contrast, defines a noun and thus is not set off by punctuation.*

CONDITIONED

In addition to embellishing or complicating the main clause, you can condition it with another clause beginning with *when, if, because, since, as,* and their many colleagues.

> *When Mr Clinton toasts Mr Jiang at the White House next week*, there will be no shortage of critics to accuse him of supping with the devil.
> *The* when *clause tells us when there will be no shortage of critics.*

> Art museums were stodgy places until 1958, *when Frank Lloyd Wright plopped a concrete cupcake on New York's Fifth Avenue.*

> *If these were to shrink,* all would suffer.

> The court refused to suppress the video and sound tapes of the Berger search *because the Constitution forbids censorship even of ill-gotten information.*

> *Since Europe opened its skies to competition last spring,* new little airlines have been taking wing.

> *As evolution goes,* from cave to restaurant is not a huge leap.

MULTIPLIED

Another variant is to combine the foregoing structures and to multiply their parts.

The number of men who consider working women to be worse mothers has dropped precipitously since 1970, but *the number of women* who think so has dropped far less sharply.

    Two main clauses joined by but.

They can make excellent eating, but *they can* also kill you.

Collective religious identity is further weakened and *individual religious autonomy further strengthened* by the separation of religion and nationality in American culture—the fact that an American may be of any religion or none and still be fully an American.

She rejected the traditional idea that women and men occupy separate spheres, in which women are naturally passive and men aggressive, and *she challenged* laws treating men and women differently, especially those designed to protect "the weaker sex."

2

OCCASIONAL SHORT FORMS

IF you do a word count of your sentences, you'll find some running thirty, forty, fifty words—too many for today's impatient reader to grasp. And I suspect you'll find only a few running ten to twenty words. Yet shorter sentences can give readers a bit of relief and draw attention to their unencumbered content.

FRAGMENTS

Sentence fragments, disallowed by rigid writers and grousing grammarians, often mimic speech and thus pick up the pace of your writing. Unexpected, they command attention, so you should draw that attention to big points and comments.

All the crusading doesn't reassure the public. *Just the opposite.*
  The full sentence would have been: Instead, it does just the opposite. *Stripping the first three words from the front and leaving the fragment drives the reader straight to the point.*

And on and on, line by line by line. The range of reference is staggering.

What users have in mind instead is a half-way house in which information is held and often processed on large, shared machines, but viewed and used on personal ones, and accessed via an open network that encourages all the collaboration, communication and information-sharing that management theorists hold so dear. *In a word, the Internet.*

Crash. Stockmarket bulls can act as brave as they like but they cannot deny the terror that this simple word strikes in their breasts.

TO START A PARAGRAPH OR POINT

Try giving your reader some relief with a five- or ten-word sentence. Like the fragment, it attracts attention. So, use it to open an argument. One of the strongest positions for the short sentence is at the beginning of a paragraph.

> *Documentary films are a worry.* First of all, there's the term "documentary" itself, which was thought clumsy by the very man who invented it, John Grierson.
>> *This short, provocative sentence prompts the reader to ask, Why?*

> *It is quite an achievement.* Though Boris Yeltsin is erratic in temperament and unsound in body, and though he had presided over a period of change in which most Russians have grown poorer, they have re-elected him.

Greenpeace used no half-measures. Claiming that old growth forests and many species of wild life were being wiped out, it called for all clear-cutting to stop, and no more new forest roads.

But others aren't so sure. "We have yet to find evidence that the introduction of new technology in schools raises test scores," says the Abell Foundation's Kate Walsh. Even some advocates, like consultant Margaret Riel, concede that test scores don't prove the case for computer networking.

TO FINISH A PARAGRAPH OR POINT

Finish a paragraph with a short declarative sentence to reinforce your point, put it in a broad perspective, or create a bridge to the next paragraph. You can also inject a bit of your humorous or skeptical self.

Ordinary people may not dine in three-star restaurants, but they have enough to eat; they may not wear Bruno Maglis, but they do not go barefoot; they may not live in Malibu, but they have roofs over their heads. *Yet it was not always thus.*
   Here, the writer is setting up the coming paragraph.

It's not that publishers are irrational or corrupt. *They're just cursed.*

But this tale of two schools shows that it is possible for poor, inner-city children to get a good education in an orderly and happy school. The things that seem to matter—good management, well-designed lessons, careful planning and high expectations—are harder to achieve than simply throwing money at schools or cutting class sizes. *But it can be done.*

It's not hard to find the winner in the Sudanese war, or in any war in Africa: it is the microbes that always emerge victorious. *Infectious disease flowers in conditions of anarchy.*

PAIRS AND TRIOS

Two or more short sentences add cadence. They also separate ideas that would otherwise be more closely linked by a conjunction in a single sentence.

> *Literature is invention. Fiction is fiction.* To call a story a true story is an insult to both art and truth.
>> *The period after invention stops the reader momentarily, abruptly separating what follows. Compare the effect with:* Literature is invention, and fiction is fiction. *Far less clear that you're dealing with two separate ideas, not two linked ones.*

Busy on two phones at once trying to stem disaster, you had no time to turn and look. *You didn't need to. You felt him.*

We detest both words. We spit them at each other with the fury of hissing geese. *We duck and dodge them.*

I came. I saw. I conquered.
> *Of course, Cicero's tricolon for Caesar.*

3

DRAMATIC FLOURISHES

AN array of flourishes can add drama to what otherwise would be common. They range from unusual punctuation, to draw attention to a word or phrase, to unusual word orders.

INTERRUPTIVE DASHES

You can occasionally use a dash to separate part of a sentence and thus draw attention to it, just as you would with a dramatic pause in speech. The dash forces your readers to momentarily reflect on what precedes the dash—and then flings them into what follows.

> New York is a city ripe with extremes—of wealth and poverty, of creative energy and rage.
>> *Without the dash, the reader would have trouble disentangling* with extremes of wealth *from* of wealth and poverty. *With it,* city ripe with extremes *is clearly articulated from the elaborations:* of wealth and poverty, of creative energy and rage.

So there's the mess — to date.

The vagabonds went on to Cuzco, an ancient city — or, rather, two or three different cities piled one on top of another.

Although Kuusisto's love for poetry can result in patches of overly self-conscious prose — "my soul crawls around like a snail exploring a piece of broken glass" — he is a powerful writer with a musical ear for language and a gift for emotional candor.

IMPERATIVES

Using the imperative is like voicing a command. Spare use grabs attention. Overuse slides into the dictatorial.

Add a bit of Iraqi intransigence, *subtract* a bit of Russian ingenuity, *throw in* a bit of UN Security Council discord, and the choice for America would have been, broadly, acquiescence or air strikes.

> *Here, the writer is asking us to act. The result: we as readers take far more note of* intransigence, ingenuity, *and* discord *than we would in the prepositional blur of* Given the combination of Iraqi intransigence, Russian ingenuity, and UN Security Council discord, ...

Trek to the tops of mountains, the sources of rivers, the earth's icebound poles.

Never mind that these charges usually evaporate under scrutiny: much of the software world is convinced that Microsoft simply does not play fair.

In Europe, where banks have long had a foot in both camps, the trading one is getting bigger: *witness* the unseemly rush by Swiss and German bankers to lay their hands on medium-sized British merchant banks with large trading outfits.

DIRECT ADDRESS

Addressing your readers, as I do throughout this little book, can make your writing more conversational and thus more personal.

If *your* stocks have risen so much in recent years that they represent an uncomfortably large portion of *your* assets, *you* should consider long-term U.S. Treasury bonds.
> *The personal pronouns* your *and* you *draw the reader into the sentence far more than would the impersonal:* If stocks have risen so much in recent years that they represent an uncomfortably large portion of an individual's assets, one should consider long-term U.S. Treasury bonds. *Compare the effect of writing* you should consider *with that of writing simply* consider, *the difference between direct address and the imperative.*

We know *you're* reading this.

Turn off a main road, wander into a village, go to see an ancient ruin, and *you* are in another country, the one where people live as they have for so many thousands of years.
> *See how the imperatives are softened?*

And *you*, with *your* western products, training, cash, clout and back-up, are fortunate compared with *your* local counterparts.

RECASTS

The recast takes the general and makes it more specific, adding power and clarity that neither could achieve on its own. Some recasts are elaborations, others definitions, still others transformations. Note that most of them are stark attachments (pages 60–63), a signal of the link between the specific and the general.

> In the past plagues were often marked by their lack of discrimination, *by the way in which they laid low vast swaths of the population with little regard for station or wealth or sex or religion.*
>
> > *The second* by *might send the reader on the wrong track of thinking that a third* by *might be coming to complete a series and that what follows the second* by *is launching something different, not similar. By sentence's end, however, it is obvious that the second* by *is a stark attachment, making more concrete the abstract* lack of discrimination.

> Unbelief remains omnipresent in American life, *the position one takes by taking no position.*

> Part of it was sheer recklessness, *a determination to plunge ahead, regardless of cars and walls and stairs.*

> Collective religious identity is further weakened and individual religious autonomy further strengthened by the separation of religion and nationality in American culture—*the fact that an American may be of any religion or none and still be fully an American.*

REVERSALS

The reversal adds to the power of what you mean by stating the same idea negatively and then positively, or sometimes vice versa. The negative to positive is stronger because it sets up an expectation.

Medical expenditures used to be small, not because doctors were cheap or hospitals were well managed but because there was only so much medicine had to offer, no matter how much you were willing to spend.

Two competing causes, and the writer tells you which is not the real one and which is, starting with the negative. Imagine the order reversed—and the loss of suspense.

The trouble is not with the facts. The trouble is that clear and honest inferences have not been drawn from the facts.

It's not so much that Wallace thinks about politics all the time as that she is continually registering its consequences on the lives of all the people she knows.

It is not that problems are not solved and questions not answered, but every solved problem generates dozens of new ones and the process gives no sign of ending.

INVERSIONS

The inversion changes common sentence order to shift a word or group of words to the emphatic opening slot and to add cadence.

So common is the experience of violent crime there that it has specialized trauma clinics for victims.

Inverting the common order for The experience of violent crime is so common there . . . *puts* so common *in front, giving it far more emphasis, and rightly submerges the flat* The experience of. . . .

Only in Asia are the Japanese doing well.

Only in the virtual world of her fiction could Austen assert control.

Nowhere is this clearer than in the world of art, where adversarial and subversive impulses have long been equated with daring and creativity.

CASCADES

The literati of the *New York Times Book Review*, seldom reined in by the short declarative sentence, often suffuse their reviews with colors, images, and sounds missing in most expository writing. So, to prove that not all your sentences need be short, here are some long ones.

So this language, with its echoes of nomads and emperors, pashas and *ghazis*, sultans and riches, and country matters, with its verbs of more than forty tenses, including the very useful one for innuendo that I wish we had, its oblique politenesses, this language with its own poetry of front- and back-rhyming vowels, this old tongue that contains within it all the past of Anatolia, is, for me, a shorthand.
   The repetition of this language *and the recast as* this old tongue *embrace, indeed contain and make more apparent, the cascade of* with its echoes, with its verbs, its oblique politenesses, *and* with its own poetry.

Ulysses is the description of a single day, the sixteenth of June 1904, a Thursday, a day in the mingled and separate lives of a number of characters walking, riding, sitting, talking, dreaming, drinking, and going through a number of minor and major physiological and philosophical actions during this one day in Dublin and the early morning hours of the next day.

Whether naturalists or cowboys, whether bluegrass aristocrats or racetrack touts, whether distinguished academics or little girls gone horse-crazy, all readers with an interest in these large, remarkable animals are bound to be fascinated by Budiansky's knowledge, by his original thinking, by the authority with which he says what many other scientists lack the wisdom or the courage to say, and by the ferocity and tenderness of his voice.

He'd been just as deeply engaged by the challenge of rocks, for instance—scouring quarries throughout the country before settling on green chert from the California Gold Country for the boulders at the head of the stream, Montana Kinnesaw for the flanks of the watercourse, clean-cut slabs of Tennessee Blue Ridge sandstone for the footpaths, and carnelian granite from South Dakota for the staggered waterfall.

FIRST AND LAST

First and last—the two parts of sentences that are most emphatic. (My first draft of this sentence was *The first and last parts of sentences are the most emphatic, the last usually the most.*) That is why it pays to see whether you can change the common order to draw attention to more important words.

Wings, legs, lungs: all were revolutionary mutations once.
*Stacking words at the front of a sentence, abruptly attaching
them to their pronoun with a colon or dash, sets them off more
starkly than does running them in.*

Propagandist, moralist, prophet—this is the rising sequence.

At least two-thirds of us are just plain rich compared to all the
rest of the human family—rich in food, rich in clothes, rich in
entertainment and amusement, rich in leisure, *rich.*
Imagine this without the exclamatory rich *standing alone at
the end.*

He reached for a word that expressed "shame, disgrace, evil
reputation, obloquy, opprobrium." His choice: *infamy.*

EXCLAMATIONS

Exclamations are stand-alone words or sentences that are often
followed by exclamation points. Reserve exclamations for highly
expressive moments—to convey humor, disgust, or exuberance.

Several years ago a scientific journal published instructions
for building a nuclear bomb. Where? *On paper!*
*This is from a satirical essay about paper, not the Internet, as
a dangerous medium. The exclamation "On paper!" shouts at
the reader, magnifying the irony of paper's danger. Imagine it
without the exclamation point.*

It will take shape, as all civilizations take shape, by the living
of it, by work and effort, by trial and error, by enterprise and ad-
venture and experience. *And by imagination!*

A cane with a shrunken human head for a handle!

Oops. There were already two Whistling Pig microbrews on the market.

INTERJECTIONS

With interjections, writers speak to the reader and themselves. Like exclamations, interjections are often followed by exclamation points. Unlike exclamations, they do not stand alone but are part of a sentence, though not grammatically tied to it.

Ah, yes, mere adultery (mundane, commonplace and in divorce, mostly a legal irrelevancy) has ended yet another military career.
　Added to the regret of Ah *is the resignation of* yes.

It goes: *gosh,* isn't Motorola amazing, all those cell phones it sells, all that total quality, all that training—*gee,* whadda company!

Ah, this getting older, however fortunate one's circumstances, is a scary business.

He is—*and how old-fashioned the words sound!*—something more than that, something resolutely indefinable, unpredictable.

HIGHLIGHTS

Italics or quotation marks can highlight a word or phrase used ironically or in an otherwise unconventional way.

Another form of diversification, *bancassurance*—tie-ups between banks and insurance companies—is still all the rage in Europe too.

> *Italics often signal a foreign word, until it is common in English.*

We are very reserved, for we have been warned not to act "green," that the city people can spot a "sucker" a mile away.

Nevertheless the simple statement stands: we are *in* the war. The irony is that Hitler knows it—and most Americans don't.

> *Italics can stress a word, as if in speech.*

The second comes from Vice-President Al Gore in 1992: "Scientists concluded—*almost unanimously*—that global warming is real and the time to act is now." (The italics are ours.)

> *Some writers use italics to highlight words in quoted material, adding a parenthetical—"(italics mine)"—or similar notation.*

4

ELEGANT REPETITIONS

REPETITION — far too often avoided — can be a powerful rhetorical device. It can bring order and balance to a sentence's parts. And it can rivet a word to the reader's frontal lobe with more impact than elegant variation ever could.

WORD

Repeating a word increases its power in the sentence by forcing the reader to reconsider its meaning and that of the words that it frames or modifies.

> However, let us not confuse the physical eye, that *monstrous* masterpiece of evolution, with the mind, an even more *monstrous* achievement.
>
> > *Adding the wonderful* monstrous *transforms the meaning of* masterpiece, *and repeating it before* achievement *sets off the contrast between* eye *and* mind *and more than doubles its power in the sentence.*

In this whole matter of War and Peace especially, we have been at *various* times and in *various* ways *false* to ourselves, *false* to each other, *false* to the facts of history and *false* to the future.

Chinatown is *ghetto*, my friends are *ghetto*, I am *ghetto*.

Already in the pace of the town, I strolled *slowly, slowly,* up the great wide ramp over the first fosse, once a moat, that day a long slope covered with flowers.
  Note with the second slowly *the tendency to read it more slowly, to stretch it out.*

ROOT

Repeating the root of a word is a way to signal different meaning and to link two ideas more strongly than would occur otherwise. Because the reader must slow down to register and consider the link, be sure you're not just being cute.

Far from discrediting liberalism, corruption is discredited by it.
  A nice turn—from discrediting *to* discredited.

It was a dramatic, not to say melodramatic, story.

Whatever it was, it caused 96% of marine species to *disappear* and dinosaurs to *appear.*

Book or music or painting, play or film, what arrests us and awes us is the realization that the *inexpressible* is arising from what is being *expressed.*

PREFIX OR SUFFIX

Repeating a prefix or suffix does more than show that words are doing the same work in a sentence. It forces the reader to see their association. This gives sentences cadence and pace.

Blind*ly*, unintentional*ly*, accidental*ly* and real*ly* in spite of ourselves, we are already a world power in all the trivial ways— in very human ways.

Common sense is fundamentally *im*moral, for the natural morals of mankind are as irrational as the magic rites that they evolved since the *im*memorial dimness of time.

Characters and authority figures pop into the story *un*announced and *un*explained.

Acts of char*ity* usually have about them a whiff of sanc*tity*.

PREPOSITION

A special case of repeating a word, a repeated preposition separates what otherwise would be the many objects of one preposition, emphasizing that they are more separate than joined. It also throws more emphasis on the preposition.

No longer do our lives depend upon the soil, the sun, the rain, or the wind; we live *by* the grace of jobs and *by* the brutal logic of jobs.

In the first series, the emphasis goes to the objects soil, sun, rain, *and* wind, *while* upon *is forgotten. In the second,* by *pulls the emphasis to* by the grace of jobs *and* by the brutal logic of jobs.

Much more could be said *in* amplification, *in* qualification, and *in* argument.

To the storyteller we turn *for* entertainment, *for* mental excitement of the simplest kind, *for* emotional participation, *for* the pleasure of traveling in some remote region in space or time.

She has an instinctive politician's gift of connecting—*to* women, *to* men, *to* old people, *to* teenagers, *to* the guy in the Staten Island deli who took her order the other weekend after she finished a five-mile run.

SOUND

Alliteration, the repetition of a sound at the beginning of two or more words in a sentence, can add poetry to the ordinary. Like all repetition, it strengthens the link between words and the attention to those linked words.

Does the *quaint quality* of *quondam* make you *quiver?*
How can you not see first the pairing of quaint *and* quality *and then tie them to* quondam *(whatever that means: but I'll bet you look it up), given the last repetition in* quiver.

Fatter capital ratios, *fancy* risk-management systems and *faster* diversification: all of these things are undoubtedly creating a *fitter* banking system.

"Baywatch," that inane *cavalcade* of *cavorting California* hunks and babes, was initially canceled after one season on NBC, but it has gone on to be seen by more people on the planet than any other entertainment show in history.

The last *leave* of *thee* takes my *weeping* eye.
  Like alliteration, assonance also repeats sound. But the sound
  is in the middle or end of words, rather than the beginning.

STRUCTURE

For the parts of sentences doing the same work—signaled by the conjunctions *and, or, but*—repeating the grammatical structures adds balance and often picks up rather than smothers the cadence. You've already seen this in many of the foregoing sections. Here, I extend it to something more than a word.

Just to be hired, he may have to take *a drug test, a lie-detector test* (though this is now limited to certain fields), and *a psychological test.*
  Article (a), *adjective* (drug, lie-detector, psychological), *noun* (test)—*with all three repeated, the list is more memorable than anything varied structures or varied words would evoke.*

There is *the same* delight in the great game of espionage, *the same* malevolent eye for human weakness, *the same* creeping sense of despair at finding oneself on the wrong side of history.

It is everywhere, *it is* cheap, and *it is*, above all, open.

White pine *is too soft*, he reasons, maple *is too sleek*, oak *is too ordinary.*

5

CREDIBLE QUOTATIONS

QUOTATION offers tremendous relief from exposition. It is also far more engaging, perhaps explaining why we'll attend to the speech-laden prose of a novel far longer than a piece of expository writing.

DIRECT

Notice how frequently the *Wall Street Journal* brings people into its stories with a quotation and the effect on the credibility of argument. Suddenly, it's no longer up to the writer to persuade. It's up to the chosen authority.

> It's no surprise that Warhol did the guest-star stunt (Halston once observed that Warhol "would go to the opening of a drawer").

> "If you see a banker jump out the window, jump after him— there's sure to be profit in it," said Voltaire.

"Trusting the government with your privacy," snorted *Wired* magazine, "is like having a Peeping Tom install your window blinds."

"In the Information Age," says education consultant Margaret Reil, "factual knowledge is plentiful. What is scarce is the intellectual work of giving value to information, of transforming information into useful knowledge systems. This is the work of communities."

INDIRECT

Indirect quotations do not guarantee exact wording, but they still command the authority quoted. Such constructions as *says that*, without quotation marks, indicate the looseness of a quotation.

Irving Clayton, a Canadian poet, observed that his countrymen are right to consider America hell; but only because Canada itself is limbo.

James Harbour, an American productivity expert, argues that by finding ways of stripping out costs without affecting quality or reliability, the Japanese could reduce costs by 40–50%.

The first shot was lobbed back in 1989, when Rushdie, four months into his Ayatollah-decreed death sentence, wrote an eviscerating review of le Carré's thriller "The Russia House"; le Carré responded *by declaring that* Rushdie had brought the "fatwa" upon himself and *criticized* him for going ahead with the paperback edition of "The Satanic Verses," suggesting that

Rushdie put a higher value on cash than on the lives of his publisher's employees.

She once told an interviewer that her Olive Oyl voice was an attempt to imitate the actress ZaSu Pitts.

OPENING WITH A QUOTATION

Opening an entire piece with a quotation sets the tone for all that follows.

"It is my duty," wrote the correspondent for The Times of London at the liberation of the Nazi death camp at Belsen, *"to describe something beyond the imagination of mankind."* That was how I felt in the summer of 1979 when I arrived in Cambodia.

"The source of my painting is the unconscious," Pollock declared, and there was no Abstract Expressionist of whom this was more clearly true.

"I think it of great importance," wrote Gouverneur Morris to George Washington in 1790, advising him on how to furnish the presidential mansion, *"to fix the taste of our country properly . . . everything about you should be substantially good and majestically plain, made to endure."*

"I still have all my arms and legs and I still have my smarts," says Gloria Mason, a 73-year-old widow from Wheaton. *"Where do I go?"* Every morning, millions of men and women—smart, curious, vibrant—face a day with no deadlines, no demands, no schedule.

SHOWING OMISSION

Ellipses (three dots) replace words you are not quoting—when the quotation is too lengthy or when your point is less apparent with the intervening words included.

> The hottest investment in Japan may well be . . . real estate.
> *An ellipsis can also cause a dramatic pause in an ordinary sentence—much like the interruptive dash (which I prefer).*

> "Our requests elicited recurrent clichés and stereotypes: Americans are given to confession. . . . Americans are puritanical. . . . Americans are obsessed with work."

> The marriage between Jane and John Clemens was "courteous, considerate and always respectful, and even deferential," their son Sam remembered; "they were always kind toward each other, but . . . there was nothing warmer."

> At least six members of the jury cried as Ryan spoke of individual victims, dramatically concluding each description by saying "the defendant killed many wives. . . . The defendant killed many children. . . . The defendant killed many grandparents."

6

CONVERSATIONAL INJECTIONS

LIKE quotations, conversational injections bring the personal into what would otherwise be impersonal and formal. They range from the wry comments to the questions and contractions that populate speech.

COMMENTS

Some words and phrases, slipped in at various points in a sentence, can reveal more of your view than mere declaration, drawing you closer to your reader.

For all their supposed mastery at putting together other peoples' businesses, investment bankers seem lousy at merging their own.

That sounds dandy, but last year was a strong one for the Canadian economy; and these high figures follow several years of low or even negative returns.

Son of one Revolutionary War hero and son-in-law of another, Allan Melvill had, *as we would say today*, good connections.

The system involves the feds in every decision to hire, which is a troubling precedent; and *of course it will make mistakes.*

QUESTIONS

Questions address readers the way imperatives do, engaging their attention. They can also add wry twists to an otherwise sober discussion. But don't sprinkle them indiscriminately—for no effect—as some journalists do. They work best at the beginning of a paragraph, creating bonds with paragraphs that precede or follow.

Could Canada really be near to breaking up after all?
Compare this with Canada could be near to breaking up, but then again it might not be.

Next: women linebackers in the National Football League?

To ensure that shareholders' assets are used wisely, it surely makes sense to pay their stewards handsomely. *But how much is that?*

QUESTIONS ANSWERED

Many writers open a paragraph with a question and keep the reader musing about possible answers through to the end. Fine, if that's the desired effect. More potent, however, is the immediate answer, especially with a fragment.

Does all this seem overdone? Well, yes.
Compare this with the common All this seems overdone.

But which countries should represent these regions. India? Pakistan says no. Brazil? Argentina says no. Nigeria? Everybody says no.

So how much can a novelist get away with? It entirely depends upon whether or not he can sustain our interest by sheer force of persuasive imaginative skill.

. . . Japan's financial system has not always been dominated by banks. Before the second world war, stock and bond markets were thriving. In the early 1930s, half of companies' capital came from issuing shares. Were these markets killed by accident or design?
    Probably a bit of both. . . .

PARENTHETICAL ASIDES

Asides plug in material not directly related to the main idea. Parentheticals can also make it easier for readers to make the leap from subject and predicate or to navigate the elements of a series.

Cheering supporters waved little Union Jacks *(provided by Blair's ever assiduous campaign staff)* and shouted "Tony! Tony!"
    What moves this comment about Blair's staff to an aside? Parentheses. Mere commas would have signaled the reader that the parenthetical material was simply adding a bit of dispensable detail.

Sterling's sci-fi protagonist goes through an implausible procedure *(albeit one based on an extrapolation of some real med-*

ical research) that restores her youth; who would not give most of their worldly goods for that?

She also deserves commendation for teaching *(for better or for worse)* the male publishing establishment a thing or two about how to sell a book.

After all, action movies, with minimal subtitles, cross linguistic barriers more easily than dramas built on dialogue and nuance. *(Boys with toys travel well, the saying goes.)*
    Sometimes an entire sentence is a parenthetical aside.

SLIPPED-IN MODIFIERS (OFTEN AS ASIDES)

Some writers put a modifier in parentheses to inject their opinion or offhandedly highlight something about what's being modified.

Two scraggly fifteen-foot palm trees in white trashcan planters have been brought in for the occasion with the *(unsuccessful)* idea of a festive touch.
    Consider this without the parentheses or without unsuccessful. *The* idea of a festive touch *suddenly becomes* the UN-SUCCESSFUL idea, *with the aside far noisier than a mere modifier.*

Durkheim offered an even more specific *(and more dynamic)* and less crystallized concept that is also a nonmaterial social fact—social currents.

Naturally, the anti-smoking ideology presumes *(wrongly)* that both conditions are true.

Like Chelsea [Clinton], they actually seem to like their dys-functional parents. Unlike her, they don't know *(or care)* much about politics, and their main civic passions are local: jobs, families, and community.

CONTRACTIONS

It used to be that contractions were all but forbidden in formal writing. Then, in the mid-1980s, they began to appear in the news—and since, more broadly. Conversational, they imbue sentences with an (often needed) air of informality.

He's just another yuppie on a power trip.
   Some editors would still turn this back to He is.

Given this climate, *it's* hardly surprising that Satan should have metamorphosed from a pitchfork-wielding fiend into the Armani-clad guy next door.

C'mon fellas—time to go all the way.

It was the best forensic advice *I'd* ever seen a candidate get, and Gore had made the most of it: *he'd* soared that night, skewering his opponents on defense policy.

7

STARK ATTACHMENTS

STARK attachments do more to distinguish the professional from the common than any other edit. And all they take is a change in position and the cutting of two or three words.

LEADING PARTS

Most writers merrily run from one independent clause to the next, either joining them in one sentence or letting them stand apart as two. Doing this, they miss the opportunity to link two ideas more closely and build a more compelling structure—one with a touch of suspense. Most leading parts could appear after the subject—less suspenseful, less emphatic.

> *Esteemed in the West as the statesman who ended the cold war*, Mr. Gorbachev is extremely unpopular in Russia, where he is blamed for allowing the Soviet Union to fall apart and for not having pushed reform of the command economy far enough.
>
> *Shortening what would otherwise have been an independent clause* (Mr. Gorbachev is esteemed . . .) *and abruptly at-*

*taching the phrase to the front of a sentence is a standard
edit that too few writers avail themselves of.*

Struck by an annual outbreak of filial sentiment, Americans
make more long-distance calls on Mother's Day than on any
other day of the year.

*Neither quite this nor altogether that, terrifically itself yet per-
petually ambiguous,* Turkey stands alone among the nations.

Like many amateur memoirs, this book may be best appreciated
by the writer, not the reader.

> A *special class of the common embellishment, with a prepo-
> sitional phrase, this one is attached to the subject that im-
> mediately follows. The example here could have been the
> common* This book is like many amateur memoirs and may
> best. . . .

INNER PARTS

Many writers habitually open their subordinate clauses with
which is, that is, who is. Taking out the pronoun and verb is a
standard edit (in the spirit of Strunk and White's "which hunt-
ing") and is one of the easiest you can make to begin building
sentences that are less ordinary.

> The PC Forum, *an annual conference that attracts some of the
> biggest names in the computer industry,* is a hard place to get
> noticed, especially if you are a relatively obscure economist.
> *The highlighted phrase could have been a dependent clause,*
> which is an annual conference. *Removing the* which is *short-
> ens the sentence and picks up the cadence by adding the elab-
> oration abruptly.*

Last year General Electric, *an American conglomerate*, earned $6.6 billion in after-tax profits by selling everything from fridges to aircraft engines.

Most writers unnecessarily introduce examples with *such as, for example, that is,* and the shorthand *i.e.* and *e.g.* Dropping those openings and replacing the surrounding commas with a pair of dashes provide variety—and pick up the cadence of your sentences.

Then along comes some external force—*a volcano, an asteroid, an ice age*—that changes all the niches and launches a mad scramble for survival.
   An ounce of example is worth a ton of abstraction.

Impressionism's essential project—*the capture of momentary effects of light*—was too insubstantial to fully engage him.

TRAILING PARTS

As with leading and inner parts, what otherwise would be an independent clause can be starkly attached as a trailing part.

The deep intrusive past was never far away—*echoed in a ruin, a habit, a village, a sight not meant to be a reminder but there all the same.*

[My house] is unadorned and functional, inexpressive and solid: it has proved this during the last war, when it went through the bombings, *escaping with some slight damage to the window frames and a few scratches which it still bears with the pride that a veteran bears the scars left by his wounds.*

And as with some other inner parts, you can remove the *who is* or *which is* from a dependent clause and attach the remaining phrase at the end with a dash or comma.

> Yet, staying at home can be the most brazen act of all. Or so we learned from Johannes Vermeer—*art's first great homebody.*
> *This might have been much flatter as* Johannes Vermeer— who was art's first great homebody.

> Hoping to jazz up vegetables' boring image, the Vegetarian Society, a British group, recently released "Hot Dinner," *an erotic public-service cinema ad bursting with rapid-fire shots of sizzling chilies and oozing peaches.*

8

DEFT CONNECTIONS

MUCH of writing is connecting words and phrases that are doing the same work—multiple subjects, verbs, modifiers, objects. And most writers connect them with conjunctions and commas in common ways. Here are some uncommon connections.

SERIES FROM SHORT TO LONG

Compound subjects and predicates and the elements of pairs or series usually appear as they come out of the writer's mind— haphazardly. Rearranging those elements from short to long and from simple to compound makes them easier for your reader to understand. Start by counting the syllables of each word—and the words of each phrase—and try arranging them from short to long. If there is another way to order the list (such as chronology or increasing importance), short to long may not apply.

> They're *smart, ambitious,* and *uncomplaining.*
>   *Compare this with the less orderly* ambitious, smart, and un-
>   complaining—*and with* uncomplaining, ambitious, and
>   smart, *inverted for an emphatic, monosyllabic finish (which
>   would be even more emphatic without the* and).

Bill Gates and his empire command *fear, respect and curiosity* in the world he helped create.

When we say *cliché, stereotype, trite pseudoelegant phrase,* and so on, we imply, among other things, that when used the first time in literature the phrase was original and had a vivid meaning.

That the cancer doctor's three main tools—*surgery, radiation and chemotherapy*—are often of so little use is no surprise: a disease caused by genetic instability requires a genetic remedy.

SERIES WITH AN EXTRA CONJUNCTION

Adding an extra conjunction to a series (usually another *and*) sets each member of the list apart and suggests that all possible members have been included—A and B and C. It can also distinguish pairings in a series—A and B, C and D, and E.

> It will take shape, as all civilizations take shape, by the living of it, by work and effort, by trial and error, by *enterprise and adventure and experience.*
> *The common form would have been* and by enterprise, adventure, and experience. *The extra* and *in the subseries, pulled from the front of the last part of the full series, gets rid of two commas and finishes with a melodic cascade.*

He can *gush and despise, revel and sneer,* as through a bifocal lens.

All through the summer there had been *rumors and waiting and hope against hope,* as there is before wars break out.

Marketing and consumer-products firms like to know who buys what—*and where and when and how.*

SERIES WITHOUT A CONJUNCTION

Dropping a conjunction has the opposite effect of adding a conjunction: creating a series that is not exhaustive, but a mere sampling of possibilities. It also makes your reader see the parts of the series as more separate than joined.

> This 20th century is *baffling, difficult, paradoxical, revolutionary.*
> *When the series ends a sentence, the final word resonates more without the* and.

> *Tattoo parlours, pawnbrokers, discounters* remain.

> It is not merely gems that De Beers is selling, but *symbols, myths, magic.*

> She spent all her time after school inside the houses of kids whose parents were *sometimes farmhands, sometimes mechanics, sometimes unemployed.*

PAIRED CONJUNCTIONS

Paired conjunctions suggest parts of equal importance and require that those parts be of the same (or at least similar) construction. They often connote something remarkable about the pairing. Common pairs: *both . . . and; not only . . . but also; either . . . or, neither . . . nor, just as . . . so.*

> But *just as* software has transformed the Internet, *so* the Internet will transform software.
> *The inversion of* software *and* Internet *to* Internet *and* software, *with a shift in tense from* has transformed *to* will transform, *is signaled by the pair* just as *and* so.

Nothing, *neither* a belief *nor* a piece of stone *nor* a memory, was wasted there, and never has been.

Today, with the globalization of American culture, it's clear that we won *not only* the cold war *but also* the battle for the world's leisure time.

Just as old does not necessarily mean feeble, *(so)* older does not necessarily mean sicker.

> *With* just as . . . so, *you can drop the word* so *if the sentence makes sense without it.*

This was a deal made *both* easier, *and* worse, by the fact that, at the eleventh hour, plummeting deficit estimates from the Congressional Budget Office gave the negotiators an extra $225 billion in projected revenues over five years to play with.

America's navy and air force tend to see a battleship as a big open space containing *either* friends, to be protected, *or* foes, to be destroyed.

STARTING WITH A CONJUNCTION

An obvious way to break a long sentence or two or three independent clauses is to make each clause a sentence. Not so obvious is keeping the conjunction at the start of the next sentence (or two). This has the added advantage of preserving the link between them. True, some of you will be aghast at such flouting of the dictates of your seventh-grade teacher. But what was common two hundred years ago (see Adam Smith's *Wealth of Nations*) is again in vogue (see *The Economist*).

I fear my memories, of which, good and bad, I have far too many. *But* lost friends are better honored with smiles than with tears. *And* having too many memories is better than having too few.

As a single sentence, this could have been a blur. Instead, the periods do their work of separating the three clauses, making them easier to grasp. And the opening conjunctions do their work of linking the three clauses.

Many people choose not to know. *But* what happens when your entire genetic closet is flung open during a routine physical?

The bosses of the world's biggest firms have great freedom to run them as they see fit, and it is almost impossible to compare their decisions to alternatives that were not—and never will be—taken. *Nor* is it easy to separate their personal contributions from plain luck.

You may open a sentence with Nor *when it follows a sentence with a negative verb phrase (generally with the word* not *in it) . . .*

A situation in a book is intensely felt because it reminds us of something that happened to us or to someone we know or knew. *Or*, again, a reader treasures a book mainly because it evokes a country, a landscape, a mode of living which he nostalgically recalls as part of his own past. *Or*, and this is the worst thing a reader can do, he identifies himself with a character in the book.

. . . or with the equivalent, as with will be unable, *which is the same as* will not be able.

SEMICOLONS

Semicolons join independent clauses without using a conjunction, binding two or more closely related ideas that are ideally parallel in construction. They cause a pause longer than a comma, shorter than a period. Some writers use them to link closely related clauses in a paragraph, to distinguish them from looser clauses and ideas.

The benefits to Africa are obvious; the benefits to America are also obvious.

A semicolon at its best, slamming together two parallel ideas and constructions.

Breeding racehorses along these lines is sensible; breeding rulers, to the modern mind, is not.

Brazilians first contemplated a new, inland capital in 1789; the name Brasilia was first suggested in 1822; yet construction did not start until 1956.

The emblems of American mass culture have infiltrated the remotest outposts: the Coca-Cola logo is on street corners from Kazakhstan to Bora-Bora; CNN emanates from television sets in more than 200 countries; there are more 7-Eleven stores in Japan than in the United States.

COLON LINKING AN EXAMPLE

Like the semicolon, the colon joins in one sentence ideas that might be treated in separate sentences, strengthening the bond between these ideas. This works well for examples.

Other little things are being changed: Japanese car makers used to paint the parts which most drivers never saw, such as the fuel tank or the drive shafts.

Then, in 1981, IBM introduced the personal computer, causing a market explosion from which emerged some of today's strongest companies: Intel, Microsoft, Compaq.

When you call your bank, you're likely to face a similar stinginess of options, but with luck they'll fit your needs: your account balance, say, or determining whether a deposit has cleared.

Soon hundreds of people were skating in concentric rings around the speakers every weekend afternoon: teen-agers in spandex, 60-year-olds in hiking shorts, Wall Street traders, Broadway dancers, Brooklyn detectives, German bankers, Brazilian nurses, Nigerian vendors, celebrities like Morgan Freeman and Margaux Hemingway bopping along next to bicycle messengers.

COLON LINKING AN ELABORATION

Colons also link elaborations, embellishments, definitions.

New platforms are often troubled early on by a nasty chicken-and-egg problem: consumers will not buy them until lots of compatible products are available, and companies will not develop compatible products until they see a market.

Here, the writer defines the nasty chicken-and-egg problem, *making certain with a colon that you read what follows as the definition.*

But Big Brother is doing his bit: in the struggle against crime, terrorism, deadbeat parents, illegal immigrants and even traf-

fic jams, the government keeps an ever-closer eye on more and more of its citizens.

As a result, American art tells the American story: Americans, like any other people, inscribe their histories, beliefs, attitudes, desires, and dreams in the images they make.

He had imparted the city's traditional philosophy toward visitors: show them no mercy.

PARALLEL CONSTRUCTIONS

Parallel structures intensify the bond between two of a sentence's joined parts and make the sentence easier to read. Any conjunction is a red flag for attending to parallel structure.

Although few realize it, Americans are generally able *to see the files kept on them, to correct mistakes, to block disclosure (sometimes, at least)* and *to learn where information has gone.*

The state, on this view, was best held to certain core functions—*providing public goods such as defense, ensuring the security of persons and property, educating citizenry, and enforcing contracts*—deemed essential for the market to flourish.

For Joyce, a Yuletide tale *"should have food in it, should have snow in it, and it should have gatherings of people, relatives that you don't like, relatives that you do like, and people that you otherwise would never have met."*

We must see and hear things, we must visualize the clothes, the rooms, the manners of an author's people.

THE VERB-FREE ELEMENT

With parallel independent clauses, you can often drop the verb from the second, leaving the reader to insert it mentally, whether singular or plural.

> Her novels *registered* these events most secretly, her letters not at all.
>> *The flatter version of this might have been* and her letters registered these events not at all. *Dropping* and *and* registered these events *shortens the sentence and picks up the cadence.*

> Premises *were* cramped, working capital scarce, infrastructure fragile and the bureaucracy tiresome.

> The trip *is* now a commodity; the tourist, a consumer; the world, a supermarket of travel opportunities trying mightily to satisfy every imaginable taste, temperament, and interest.

> She *supplied* the facts and statistics, I the philosophy and rhetoric, and, together, we have made arguments that stood unshaken through the storms of long years; arguments that no one has answered.

9

ONE-SYLLABLE OPENINGS

SENTENCES obviously get off to a faster start with a one-syllable opening than with words of two or more syllables. And successions of one-syllable openings can (occasionally) bind a paragraph more tightly. Rely on your ear—and restraint—to use these openings for best effect. For they swiftly descend into the common.

IT

Starting a sentence with *It* is generally to be avoided, as in *It is Johnson who damaged . . .* , *It can now be stated with certainty that . . .* , or *It goes without saying that . . .* (why say it?). The reason: something deserving emphasis at the start of a sentence becomes submerged by the fatty opening. But an opening *it* can get a paragraph or entire piece off to a fast, emphatic, monosyllabic start.

> *It* is with noble sentiments that bad literature gets written.
> *Notice how clean this opening is.*

It is not at all hard to see how the American economy could support a much larger medical sector; it is, however, very hard to see how the U.S. Government will manage to pay for its share of that sector's costs.

It is wartime; no new labor is coming in from the old countries across the seas.

It is that old, old issue with those old, old battered labels—the issue of Isolationism versus Internationalism.

THERE

Opening with *There is* or *There are* is one of the most natural ways of starting a sentence in speech and thus in print. So natural that it tires from overuse. So, much like the opening *It*, the opening *There* is something generally to avoid. Reserve it for the special needs of conversational punch and variety.

> *There* is little artistic relevance in classifying rap music, a definite and unique rap form, as poetry.
> *Starting with* There *gives this sentence an easy, natural flow. The alternative*—Classifying rap music, a definite and unique rap form, as poetry has little artistic relevance—*is bumpier.*

There were many stories of courage that night.

There may have been another factor: Fuchs was complaining.

There has been no post-revolutionary toppling of statues and icons.

THIS

As a pronoun for something that has just been mentioned or is about to be, *This* is one of those useful monosyllables for opening a sentence. And as a pronoun, it's essential.

This is a good day to take a close look at a famous speech.
This forward reference is a common opening sentence for expository writing of all types. This *refers to what follows:* a good day. *(The same goes for its plural,* these.*)*

This would be wizardry indeed.

This is quite a declaration.

This contradiction necessitates that we speak of money euphemistically or keep quiet.

THAT

As a pronoun for something just mentioned, *That* is another of those useful monosyllables. But as with the backward reference for *This*, be sure that it is perfectly clear what *That* refers to.

That is why the best outcome from Kyoto would have been a modest, politically workable agreement to curb emissions of greenhouse gases pending further study.
A pronoun doing its duty: standing for many more words preceding it.

That will teach them to disrespect their bodies.

That leaves Mr. Mbeki treading a delicate line between keeping them happy and suffocating the businesses on which he knows full well economic success depends.

That, in fact, is part of the problem: the golfer has all the time in the world to think.

WHAT

The structure of this can get confusing, depending on whether *What* is a pronoun or adjective.

What a shock it must be for Koreans to discover that what they thought was a rich, rapidly growing homeland with near-perfect job security is in fact teetering on the edge of bankruptcy.
   Adjective modifying shock.

What they didn't know proved liberating.

What we hear is not necessarily what is said.

What made Max Beerbohm's malice merry was its distant, generally impersonal, and always playful quality.

EXEMPLARY SENTENCES

Clive Crook

"EUROPE'S GAMBLE"

Repetition of M sound —

IN May 1998, Europe's governments will make the most momentous decision about Europe's future since the creation of the Common Market in 1958: they will say which countries will be founder members of the new monetary union. Recently they underlined their determination to stick to the timetable laid down in the Maastricht treaty. The meeting next May will decide not only which countries are to go forward in the first wave but also the parties to be fixed "irrevocably" from January 1st, 1999, when EMU comes into force.

Colon linking an example

Highlight

Opening embellishment —

—Only a few months ago, the monetary union project seemed to be faltering, to the relief of Britain's Labour government, among others, who would rather the subject went away for a few years. Now it is back on schedule, its momentum renewed. At last the fact is sinking in: EMU is coming—a "wide" EMU, including Italy, Spain and Portugal—

Closing clause comments

Highlight

Dashed inner part

and it is coming whether Europe's voters like it or not.

On the whole, and to the extent that they have a view one way or the other, they seem not to like it. This should count for something, you might think, given that the EU's 15 countries are democracies.

But Europe's politicians appear to think otherwise: so far they have made next to no effort to educate their electorates on the benefits and drawbacks of what is proposed. Why? Because this is not (or not yet) an issue that divides people neatly along party-political lines. It cuts across those lines—and no politician in Europe needs reminding of what happened to Britain's Tories when they put their disagreement on this subject frankly before the public. As a result, the lack of political preparation for the EMU is almost total. This is matched by an equally comprehensive lack of economic preparation.

Does this matter? Yes. Because of it, the benefits of monetary union will be smaller than they might have been and the drawbacks bigger, possibly catastrophic. A project that makes good sense in principle has become far, far riskier than it ever need have been. Why run this danger? It cannot be right, you might think, to say that there has been no preparation for EMU: only consider the time and effort that Europe's governments have devoted to the Maastricht "convergence criteria." True, plenty of time and effort have been spent—but to very little useful effect.

The trouble with the Maastricht criteria is

Margin annotations (left): Opening embellishment · Direct address · Complicated clause · Opening conjunction · Question answered with fragment · Conditioned clause · Repetition of "preparation"

Margin annotations (right): Opening "this" · Colon linking an elaboration. · Parenthetical aside · Repetition of P sound · Opening "It" · Direct address · Colon linking an elaboration · Interruptive dash

not mainly that they have been fiddled (though they have been outlandishly and will be even more so before next May) but that they were beside the point in the first place. The treaty called for four main kinds of convergence: on inflation, interest rates, budget deficits and public debt.

These rules were, and remain, a mixture of the unnecessary, the irrelevant and the counter-productive. But what matters far more are two convergence criteria that the treaty does not mention at all: labour-market flexibility and national responses to changes in interest rates. When EMU comes into operation, governments will no longer be able to use changes in monetary policy to stabilize their national economies—cutting interest rates and depreciating their currencies in recessions, raising rates and appreciating their currencies in booms.

—This is a big loss. In Europe at present monetary policy shoulders the larger part of the burden of adjustment to economic fluctuations. Once national monetary policy is abolished for this purpose, the burden must fall elsewhere: partly on fiscal policy and partly on the labour market. Bizarrely, Europe's governments say they will not rely much on fiscal policy. (Germany's proposed "stability pact", which makes the Maastricht budget-deficit criterion a permanent rule, seeks to formalise this self-denying, self-destructive ordinance.) So Europe's nations will be left with only changes in wages to adjust to swings of the economic cycle. Therefore, if France, say, should suffer an economic downturn once EMU is up and running, the only remedy for unemployment will be lower wages.

In flexible, deregulated labour markets (such as America's), a small reduction in wages is enough to spur employment powerfully; in rigid, highly regulated ones, bigger pay-cuts are required. Europe's labour markets are the most rigid in the world. Unemployment rises more in Europe than in America during economic downturns. Putting this right is essential if the political and economic risks of EMU are to be minimized. But governments are doing almost nothing and initiatives such as the "social chapter" threaten to make the problem worse. The other missing convergence criterion is responsiveness to interest rates. When Europe's new central bank puts interest rates up in order to reduce inflationary pressures across the EU, the precise effect will depend on the fine structure of national financial systems. For instance, the effect will be smaller in countries where housing finance is arranged mainly on a fixed-rate basis rather than on a variable-rate basis. In this way and others, when the central bank changes its interest rate the effect will differ in strength from country to country: a change sufficient to modern demand in one country may be enough to induce a recession in another. Sensible governments planning for EMU would have addressed this by now.

The lack of inquiry and debate about EMU in Europe has been lamentable. Britain has had a debate, of sorts—but not

Opening embellishment

Semicolon links parallel clauses

Common direct form

Common direct form

Opening conjunction

Highlight

Repetition of "convergence criterion"

Opening embellishment

Parallel construction

Colon linking an example

Common conditioned form

Common direct form

Repetition of L sound

Interruptive dash

an illuminating one. The Tories divide into warring camps, one for EMU and the other against, neither side caring in the least about details or circumstances. Elsewhere there has been hardly any debate at all. Yet whether EMU is a success or a failure turns entirely on the details and the circumstances. Far too little is being done to make it the success it could be or to minimize the dangers. When you consider how steep the costs of failure might be—not merely a needlessly deep recession nor even the collapse of an ill-constructed monetary union but the coming apart of the EU itself—these omissions are nothing short of outrageous. And 1998 will show them to be so.

Common direct form

Short form to start a point

Repetition of "details and circumstances"

Dashed inner part

Repetition of ēē sounds and "ssion" sounds

Short form to finish paragraph

Opening conjunction

Permission to reprint
granted by *The Economist*

Michiko Kakutani

"MASTER OF HIS DOMAIN"

THE funniest man in America isn't on television. He doesn't do stand-up or talk shows or American Express ads. He doesn't make silly faces or rude noises. He doesn't try to spin his own indiscretions into pretentious art. His jokes aren't about "nothing"; they're not even about himself. Indeed, his specialty is making black comedy out of such unfunny objects as high finance and gutter journalism, Hollywood tunnel vision and Washington doublespeak, human vanity and greed.

—— Over a five-decade career, Larry Gelbart, 72, has wielded his virtuoso comedy skills in radio, TV, film and theater and worked with everyone from Bob Hope and Sid Caesar to John Belushi and Bill Murray. Along the way, he has proven himself a master of virtually every comedic form, but whether it's a vaudeville takeoff on Plautus ("A Funny Thing Happened on the Way to the Forum"), gender-bending farce ("Tootsie"), political

Margin annotations: Contractions; Parallel construction; Highlight; Semicolon contractions; Parallel pairs; Added conjunction; Opening embellishment; Parallel pairs; Parenthetical asides

satire ("Mastergate") or half-hour television ("M*A*S*H"), two constants can be found: a consummate craftsman's love of language and a disappointed idealist's rage at a corrupt, tawdry, sanctimonious and hypocritical world. Those same two qualities animate Gelbart's new book of essays, "Laughing Matters" (due next month from Random House), and they also percolate throughout his conversation, along with lots of puns, aphorisms and jokes.

The man is not only a compulsive writer—he's currently working on a musical stage version of "A Star is Born," a film version of "Chicago," a remake of the Peter Cook–Dudley Moore comedy "Bedazzled" and an HBO series about a Beverly Hills plastic surgeon—but he's also a reflexive ad-libber, a hyperkinetic talker who says it would be nice to have "a dimmer" in his brain. In his later work, Gelbart has skewered the tabloid wars ("Weapons of Mass Distraction"), corporate takeovers ("Barbarians at the Gate") and Hollywood venality ("City of Angels"), and when he talks about comedy writing, it quickly becomes clear that he is equally indignant about the state of his own art. As Gelbart sees it, people have become increasingly cynical about politics, increasingly resigned to being ineffectual receivers of bad news. And humor, in turn, has grown increasingly escapist, juvenile and bitchy. In more and more movie comedies, he observes, "with has been replaced by wind," and on television, the serious themes once examined by shows like "All

Margin annotations: Colon links example; Common multiplied form; Repetition of C sound; Series short to long; Highlight; Parenthetical aside; Interruptive dash; Interruptive dash; Indirect quotation; Highlights; Parenthetical asides; Repetition; Opening conjunction; Parallel structure; Direct quotation

in the Family," and "M*A*S*H" have given way to the stupid bedroom and bathroom jokes of shows like "Veronica's Closet." "It's all about did she, will she or won't she," he says. "It's like Doris Day on speed. It's all about doing it and each other's pee-pees." He says he thinks it's great that a show as "hip and offbeat" as "Seinfeld" is a hit but adds that its wackiness "is a studied wacky—they're like professional kooks." He calls "Def Comedy Jam" "a miracle of bad taste . . . riot comedy, not a comedy riot," and says of "Friends," "It's just attitude, and 'tude is easier to write than jokes." Gelbart does give high marks to "The X-Files" ("The funniest guy on TV is David Duchovny—he's always saying things that are very flippant in situations that are anything but that"), C-Span ("I like aliens of any sort") and "Politically Incorrect" ("It reminds me of the old days, when people were more outspoken"). Certainly comedy writing has changed considerably since Gelbart began working back in the 40's and 50's. Among the developments that Gelbart says have changed his craft are a global film market that discounts verbal comedy and the comedy of ideas, an audience that has lost "the ability to be ashamed," and shorter attention spans that make the sort of story-based humor once practiced by comics like Danny Thomas harder to sustain. At the same time, he believes, audiences' standards have slipped: forget finely crafted jokes and sophisticated wordplay—these days, an embarrassing revelation or a few dirty words are enough to get a reaction. "You really had to earn the laughter in the old days," Gelbart says. "Now we've got shock in place of wit, shock even in place of jokes. And some people aren't even shocked: they're just laughing because, 'Hey, this guy talks just like me.'"

—In addition, Gelbart argues, TV writing has grown more solipsistic: whereas television once attracted people trained in radio, film and theater, it's now the province of lifelong couch potatoes with a fondness for inside jokes. And on sitcoms, those jokes are increasingly crafted by committees. "There's a custom out here now called table writing," he says. "A draft will be prepared by one or two writers, and the staff will sit around a table and try to get in as many new lines as possible. It is not an art being practiced here. It is a product being manufactured to as rigid a set of standards as getting all the right ingredients inside a bottle of Coca-Cola." Although such sharply held views about Hollywood and big business have fueled some of Gelbart's most recent and savage work, he says it's becoming harder to write satire when reality itself feels so surreal.

— In a time when the President's sex life is front-page news and disgraced ambassadors are being exhumed at Arlington, he says, the most one can do is "stay about five seconds ahead of the curve." "A large part of you doesn't want to be funny about it at all," he adds. "A large part of you wants to cry. Sure, my stuff has gotten darker in recent years, but life's gotten darker. As one gets ready for the final curtain, the process enables you to stop

Margin annotations:
- Direct quotation
- Repetition of "shock"
- Exclamation
- Opening embellishment
- Colon linking an example
- Opening conjunction
- Direct quotation
- Parallel structure
- Passive voice
- Indirect quotation
- Opening embellishment
- Parallel structure

denying as much as you have about where you're going and what's around you while you're still here. And even if that weren't the process, you have to admit, these are pretty scandalous times. I think reporters have become the new satirists."

Opening conjunction

Permission to reprint granted
by the *New York Times*

SOURCES

1. COMMON FORMS

Direct

"Those Magical Mushrooms," *The Economist* 345, no. 8048 (20 December 1997): 93.

Bob Morris, "Let Them Eat Elsewhere," *New York Times Magazine*, 19 October 1997, sec. 6, p. 91.

Floyd Norris, "Korean Crisis: Blame the Lenders," *New York Times*, 14 December 1997, sec. 3, p. 1.

"Poetic Injustice," *The Economist* 345, no. 8048 (20 December 1997): 129.

Embellished

Alabama Isn't So Different," *The Economist* 345, no. 8039 (18 October 1997): 27.

Tina Rosenberg, "To Hell and Back," *New York Times Magazine*, 28 December 1997, sec. 6, p. 32.

"Ambiguity's Path to Murder," *The Economist* 345, no. 8039 (18 October 1997): 47.

"Why Pagodas Don't Fall Down," *The Economist* 345, no. 8048 (20 December 1997): 121.

Complicated

Judith Shulevitz, "Prematurely Correct," *New York Times Book Review*, 14 December 1997, sec. 7, p. 18.

Isabelle de Courtivron, "Rebel without a Cause," *New York Times Book Review*, 14 December 1997, sec. 7, p. 14.

"Those Magical Mushrooms," *The Economist* 345, no. 8098 (20 December 1997): 95.

"The Birth of a New Species," *The Economist* 339, no. 7967 (25 May 1996): 4.

Conditioned

"Greeting the Dragon," *The Economist* 345, no. 8040 (25 October 1997): 15.

"A Beauty Is Born," *The Economist* 345, no. 8040 (25 October 1997): 94.

"Crash, Dammit," *The Economist* 345, no. 8039 (18 October 1997): 13.

Max Frankel, "A Case of Sheep v. Coyotes," *New York Times Magazine*, 21 December 1997, sec. 6, p. 30.

"Glittering Gadfly," *The Economist* 346, no. 8054 (7 February 1998): 65.

"Watching Where You Eat," *The Economist* 346, no. 8053 (31 January 1998): 87.

Multiplied

Sarah Boxer, "One Casualty of the Women's Movement: Feminism," *New York Times*, 14 December 1997, sec. 4, p. 3.

"Those Magical Mushrooms," *The Economist* 345, no. 8048 (20 December 1997): 93.

Jack Miles, "Religion Makes a Comeback (Belief to Follow)," *New York Times Magazine*, 7 December 1997, sec. 6, p. 56.

Jeffrey Rosen, "The New Look of Liberalism on the Court," *New York Times Magazine*, 5 October 1997, sec. 6, p. 60.

2. OCCASIONAL SHORT FORMS

Fragments

Robert J. Samuelson, "The Attack Culture," *Washington Post*, 12 March 1997, sec. A, p. 19.

Louis Menand, "How Eliot Became Eliot," *New York Review of Books* 54, no. 8 (15 May 1997): 27.

"Back to the Garage," *The Economist* 339, no. 7967 (25 May 1996): 5.

"If Wall Street Falters," *The Economist* 340, no. 7973 (6 July 1996): 119.

To start a paragraph or point

Stanley Kauffmann, *Distinguishing Features* (Baltimore: Johns Hopkins University Press, 1994), p. 10.

"Too Far on Forfeitures," *New York Times*, 26 June 1996, sec. A, p. 18.

"A Surprise in the Woods," *The Economist* 344, no. 8026 (19 July 1997): p. 31.

What's Going On (Washington, D.C.: Benton Foundation, 1997), p. 10.

To finish a paragraph or point

Paul Krugman, "Does Getting Old Cost Society Too Much?" *New York Times Magazine*, 9 March 1997, sec. 6, p. 60.

James Surowiecki, "The Publisher's Curse," *New York Times Magazine*, 31 May 1998, sec. 6, p. 24.

"Time for Reform?" *The Economist* 345, no. 8044 (22 November 1997): 65.

Jeffrey Goldberg, "Our Africa," *New York Times Magazine*, 2 March 1997, sec. 6, p. 35.

Pairs and trios

Vladimir Nabokov, *Lectures on Literature* (1980; New York: Harcourt Brace Jovanovich, 1982), p. 5.

Michael Lewis, *Liar's Poker* (New York: Penguin, 1989), p. 13.

Henry R. Luce, *The American Century* (New York: Farrar and Rinehart, 1941), p. 22.

Cicero, on Julius Caesar.

3. DRAMATIC FLOURISHES

Interruptive dashes

Hubert B. Herring, "Diary," *New York Times*, 18 May 1997, sec. 4, p. 2.

Henry R. Luce, *The American Century* (New York: Farrar and Rinehart, 1941), p. 15.

Paul Berman, "Biker Days," *New Yorker Magazine* 71, no. 22 (31 July 1995): 78.

Michiko Kakutani, "Planet of the Blind: Passing as a Person Who Can See," *New York Times*, 23 December 1997, sec. E, p. 6.

Imperatives

"America the Unmighty," *The Economist* 345, no. 8045 (29 November 1997): 17.

Edwin Dobb, "Where the Good Begins," *Harper's* 297, no. 1778 (July 1998): 60.

"The Tyranny of Success," in *Survey of the Software Industry* (insert), *The Economist* 339, no. 7967 (25 May 1996): 9.

"System Failure," in *International Banking Survey, The Economist* 339, no. 7963 (27 April 1996): 6.

Direct address

James K. Glassman, washingtonpost.com, 11 June 1997.

"We Know You're Reading This," *The Economist* 338, no. 7952 (10 February 1996): 27.

Mary Lee Settle, *Turkish Reflections: A Biography of a Place* (1991; New York: Simon & Schuster, 1992), p. xvii.

"The Next Revolution," in *Survey: Business in Eastern Europe, The Economist* 345, no. 8044 (22 November 1997): 3.

Recasts

Andrew Sullivan, "When Plagues End," *New York Times Magazine*, 10 November 1996, sec. 6, p. 55.

Jack Miles, "Religion Makes a Comeback. (Belief to Follow)," *New York Times Magazine*, 7 December 1997, sec. 6, p. 58.

Michiko Kakutani, Planet of the Blind: Passing as a Person Who Can See," *New York Times*, 23 December 1997, sec. E, p. 6.

Jack Miles, "Religion Makes a Comeback. (Belief to Follow)," *New York Times Magazine*, 7 December 1997, sec. 6, p. 56.

Reversals

Paul Krugman, "Does Getting Old Cost Society Too Much?" *New York Times Magazine*, 9 March 1997, sec. 6, p. 60.

Henry R. Luce, *The American Century* (New York: Farrar and Rinehart, 1941), p. 7.

Vivian Gornick, "An American Exile in America," *New York Times Magazine*, 2 March 1997, sec. 6, p. 28.

Primo Levi, *Other People's Trades* (London: Michael Joseph, 1989; London: Abacus, 1990), p. 27.

Inversions

"The End of the Miracle?" *The Economist* 345, no. 8047 (13 December 1997): 18.

"Lean enough?" *The Economist* 338, no. 7952 (10 February 1996): 60.

Kevin Barry, "Still Clueless," *New York Times Book Review*, 7 December 1997, sec. 7, p. 46.

Michiko Kakutani, "To Hell with Him," *New York Times Magazine*, 7 December 1997, sec. 6, p. 38.

Cascades

Mary Lee Settle, *Turkish Reflections: A Biography of a Place* (1991; New York: Simon & Schuster, 1992), p. 35.

Vladimir Nabokov, *Lectures on Literature* (1980; New York: Harcourt Brace Jovanovich, 1982), p. 285.

Elizabeth Marshall Thomas, "Horse Sense," *New York Review of Books* 44, no. 8 (15 May 1997): 11.

Lawrence Weschler, "When Fountainheads Collide," *New Yorker Magazine* 73, no. 38 (8 December 1997): 67.

First and last

"The Birth of a New Species," in *Survey of the Software Industry* (insert), *The Economist* 339, no. 7967 (25 May 1996): 3.

Vladimir Nabokov, *Lectures on Literature* (1980; New York: Harcourt Brace Jovanovich, 1982), p. 3.

Henry R. Luce, *The American Century* (New York: Farrar and Rinehart, 1941), p. 5.

William Safire, "Day of Infamy," *New York Times Magazine*, 7 December 1997, sec. 6, p. 30.

Exclamations

Michael Kinsley, Op-Ed, *Washington Post*, 16 April 1997, sec. A, p. 17.

Henry R. Luce, *The American Century* (New York: Farrar and Rinehart, 1941), p. 34.

David Wallace, "Lost Luggage," *New York Times Magazine*, 21 December 1997, sec. 6, p. 19.

Daniel D'Ambrosio, "Leggo My Logo," *New York Times Magazine*, 5 October 1997, sec. 6, p. 23.

Interjections

Richard Cohen, "The Army's Search and Self-Destroy Mission," *Washington Post*, 5 June 1997, sec. A, p. 21.

"Tough at the Top," *The Economist*, 338, no. 7947 (6 January 1996): 47.

Mary Cantwell, "Still at Work on a Self," *New York Times Magazine*, 9 March 1997, sec. 6, p. 57.

James Baldwin, *Notes of a Native Son* (Boston: Beacon, 1955, 1957, 1983), p. 15.

Highlights

"System Failure," in *International Banking Survey, The Economist* 339, no. 7963 (27 April 1996): 6.

Richard Wright, *12 Million Black Voices* (New York: Viking, 1941), p. 99.

Henry R. Luce, *The American Century* (New York: Farrar and Rinehart, 1941), p. 9.

"Plenty of Gloom," *The Economist* 345, no. 8048 (20 December 1997): 20.

4. ELEGANT REPETITIONS

Word

Vladimir Nabokov, *Lectures on Literature* (1980; New York: Harcourt Brace Jovanovich, 1982), p. 3.

Henry R. Luce, *The American Century* (New York: Farrar and Rinehart, 1941), p. 6.

Henry Han Xi Lau, "I Was a Member of the Kung Fu Crew," *New York Times Magazine*, 19 October 1997, sec. 6, p. 54.

Mary Lee Settle, *Turkish Reflections: A Biography of a Place* (1991; New York: Simon & Schuster, 1992), p. 17.

Root

"Stop the Rot," *The Economist* 350, no. 8102 (16 *January* 1999): 19.

Primo Levi, *Other People's Trades* (London: Michael Joseph, 1989; London: Abacus, 1990), p. 27.

"The Birth of a New Species," in *Survey of the Software Industry* (insert), *The Economist* 339, no. 7967 (25 May 1996): 3.

Stanley Kauffmann, "sex, lies, and videotape," in *Distinguishing Features* (Baltimore: Johns Hopkins University Press, 1994), p. 133.

Prefix or suffix

Henry R. Luce, *The American Century* (New York: Farrar and Rinehart, 1941), p. 33.

Vladimir Nabokov, *Lectures on Literature* (1980; New York: Harcourt Brace Jovanovich, 1982), p. 372.

Michael Parfit, "Breathless," *New York Times Book Review*, 7 December 1997, sec. 7, p. 24.

Michael Lewis, "Heartless Donors," *New York Times Magazine*, 14 December 1997, sec. 6, p. 46.

Preposition

Richard Wright, *12 Million Black Voices* (New York: Viking, 1941), p. 100.
Henry R. Luce, *The American Century* (New York: Farrar and Rinehart, 1941), p. 15.
Vladimir Nabokov, *Lectures on Literature* (1980; New York: Harcourt Brace Jovanovich, 1982), p. 5.
Elisabeth Bumiller, "The Politics of Personality," *New York Times Magazine*, 2 November 1997, sec. 6, p. 38.

Sound

Merriam-Webster Online Edition of Explorer (m~w.com), 16 December 1997.
"System failure," in *International Banking Survey*, *The Economist* 339, no. 7963 (27 April 1996): 6.
Michiko Kakutani, "Taking Out the Trash," *New York Times Magazine*, 8 June 1997, sec. 6, p. 34.
William Shakespeare, *Richard II* 1.2.74.

Structure

"We Know You're Reading This," *The Economist* 338, no. 7952 (10 February 1996): 27.
Robert Harris, "I, Spy," *New Yorker Magazine* 73, no. 15 (9 June 1997): 98.
"The Birth of a New Species," in *Survey of the Software Industry* (insert), *The Economist* 339, no. 7967 (25 May 1996): 4.
Witold Rybczynski, "This New House," *New York Review of Books* 44, no. 8 (15 May 1997): 24.

5. CREDIBLE QUOTATIONS

Direct

Michiko Kakutani, "The United States of Andy," *New York Times Magazine*, 17 November 1996, sec. 6, p. 34.
"Coping with the Ups and Downs," in *International Banking Survey*, *The Economist* 339, no. 7963 (27 April 1996): 3.
"We Know You're Reading This," *The Economist* 338, no. 7947 (10 February 1996): p. 27.
What's Going On (Washington, D.C.: Benton Foundation, 1997), p. 10.

Indirect

"Limbo, Seen from Hell," *The Economist* 339, no. 7964 (4 May 1996): 73.

"Lean Enough?" *The Economist* 338, no. 7952 (10 February 1996): 59.

Vanessa Friedman, "Fax from London," in Talk of the Town, *New Yorker Magazine* 73, no. 38 (8 December 1997): 37.

Rick Lyman, "Mae Questel, 89, behind Betty Boop and Olive Oyl," *New York Times*, 8 January 1998, sec. B, p. 9.

Opening with a quotation

John Pilger, "America's Long Affair with Pol Pot," *Harper's* 297, no. 1778 (July 1998): 15.

Robert Hughes, "American Visions," *Time*, special issue, May 1997, 37.

Ibid.

Roxanne Roberts, "Holiday Park's Senior Class," *Washington Post*, 2 June 1997, sec. D, p. 1.

Showing omission

"Get Real," *The Economist* 342, no. 8009 (22 March 1997): 97.

"How the World Sees Us" (introduction to a special issue of the *New York Times Magazine*), 8 June 1997, sec. 6, p. 37.

Andrew Hoffman, *Inventing Mark Twain: The Lives of Samuel Langhorne Clemens* (New York: Morrow, 1997), p. 3.

Lois Romano, "McVeigh Jurors Sob at Victims' Pain," *Washington Post*, 5 June 1997, sec. A, p. 15.

6. CONVERSATIONAL INJECTIONS

Comments

"Eviction in the City," *The Economist* 342, no. 7964, no. 8007 (8 March 1997): 85.

"Limbo, Seen from Hell," *The Economist* 339, no. 7964 (4 May 1996): 74.

Andrew Delbanco, "The Great Leviathan," *New York Review of Books* 44, no. 8 (15 May 1997): 18.

"We Know You're Reading This," *The Economist* 338, no. 7952 (10 February 1996): 27.

Questions

"Shaking Canada," *The Economist* 337, no. 7937 (21 October 1995): 41.

"A Wealth of Working Women," *The Economist* 339, no. 7969 (8 June 1996): 28.

"The Need for Greed," *The Economist* 339, no. 7964 (4 May 1996): 80.

Questions answered

Robert J. Samuelson, "Telephone Straddle," *Washington Post*, 14 May 1997, sec. A, p. 21.

"To Bury or to Praise," *The Economist* 337, no. 7937 (21 October 1995): 27.

"The Philosopher's Pupil," *The Economist* 334, no. 7897 (14 January 1995): 77.

"A Cautionary Tale," in *Survey: Japanese Finance The Economist* 343, no. 8023 (28 June 1997): 5.

Parenthetical asides

John Cassidy, "Rosy-Digited Dawn," *New Yorker Magazine* 73, no. 11 (12 May 1997): 7.

Paul Krugman, "Does Getting Old Cost Society Too Much?" *New York Times Magazine*, 9 March 1997, sec. 6, p. 60.

Karen Lehrman, "The Original Valley Girl," *New York Times Book Review*, 4 January 1998, sec. 7, p. 27.

Michiko Kakutani, "The Culture Zone," *New York Times Magazine*, 8 June 1997, sec. 6, p. 32.

Slipped-in modifiers (often as asides)

Robert Klitgaard, *Tropical Gangsters* (New York: Basic Books, 1990), p. 2.

George Ritzer, *Sociological Theory*, 4th ed. (New York: McGraw-Hill, 1992), p. 86.

Robert J. Samuelson, "Anti-Smoking Hysteria," *Washington Post*, 23 April 1997, sec. A, p. 21.

Ian Fisher, "The No-Complaints Generation," *New York Times Magazine*, 5 October 1997, sec. 6, p. 68.

Contractions

Michiko Kakutani, "To Hell with Him." *New York Times Magazine*, 7 December 1997, sec. 6, p. 38.

Ibid., p. 37.

William Safire, "Day of Infamy," *New York Times Magazine*, 7 December 1997, sec. 6, p. 32.

Joe Klein, "Learning to Run," *New Yorker Magazine* 73, no. 38 (8 December 1997): 53.

7. STARK ATTACHMENTS

Leading parts

Alessandra Stanley, "From Perestroika to Pizza: Gorbachev Stars in TV Ad," *New York Times*, 3 December 1997, sec. A, p. 1.

"The Death of Distance," in *A Survey of Telecommunications* (insert), *The Economist* 336, no. 7934 (30 September 1995): 5.

Mary Lee Settle, *Turkish Reflections: A Biography of a Place* (1991; New York: Simon & Schuster, 1992), p. ix.

Wendy Kaminer, "Fool for Love," *New York Times Book Review*, 14 December 1997, sec. 7, p. 32.

Inner parts

"The Tyranny of Success," in *Survey of the Software Industry* (insert), *The Economist* 339, no. 7967 (25 May 1996): 9.

"The Need for Greed," *The Economist* 339, no. 7964 (4 May 1996): 80.

"The Birth of a New Species," in *Survey of the Software Industry* (insert), *The Economist* 339, no. 7967 (25 May 1996): 9.

Simon Schama, "Cézanne's Mission," *New Yorker Magazine* 72, no. 16 (17 June 1996): 92.

Trailing parts

Mary Lee Settle, *Turkish Reflections: A Biography of a Place* (1991; New York: Simon & Schuster, 1992), p. 26.

Primo Levi, *Other People's Trades* (London: Michael Joseph, 1989; London: Abacus, 1990), p. 1.

Deborah Solomon, "The Stay at Home Life as Muse," *New York Times*, 20 March 1997, sec. C, p. 1.

David Wallis, "The Joy of Vegetables," *New York Times Magazine*, 12 July 1998, sec. 6, p. 13.

8. DEFT CONNECTIONS

Series from short to long

Ian Fisher, "The No-Complaints Generation," *New York Times Magazine*, 5 October 1997, sec. 6, p. 68.

"The Tyranny of Success," in *Survey of the Software Industry* (insert), *The Economist* 339, no. 7967 (25 May 1996): 9.

Vladimir Nabokov, *Lectures on Literature* (1980); New York: Harcourt
  Brace Jovanovich, 1982, p. 346.
Nicholas Wade, "Can the Common Cold Cure Cancer?" *New York Times
  Magazine*, 21 December 1997, sec. 6, p. 34.

Series with an extra conjunction

Henry R. Luce, *The American Century* (New York: Farrar and Rinehart,
  1941), p. 34.
Stanley Kauffmann, *Distinguishing Features* (Baltimore: Johns Hopkins
  University Press, 1994), p. 15.
Mary Lee Settle, *Turkish Reflections: A Biography of a Place* (1991; New
  York: Simon & Schuster, 1992), p. 29.
"We Know You're Reading This," *The Economist* 338, no. 7947 (10
  February 1996): 27.

Series without a conjunction

Henry R. Luce, *The American Century* (New York: Farrar and Rinehart,
  1941), p. 29.
"The Mall of Dreams," *The Economist* 339, no. 7964 (4 May 1996): 23.
"Glass with Attitude," *The Economist* 345, no. 8048 (20 December 1997):
  113.
Vivian Gornick, "An American Exile in America," *New York Times
  Magazine*, 2 March 1997, sec. 6, p. 28.

Paired conjunctions

"The Birth of a New Species," in *Survey of the Software Industry* (insert),
  The Economist 339, no. 7967 (25 May 1996): 4.
Mary Lee Settle, *Turkish Reflections: A Biography of a Place* (1991; New
  York: Simon & Schuster, 1992), p. 16.
Michiko Kakutani, "Taking Out the Trash," *New York Times Magazine*, 8
  June 1997, sec. 6, p. 34.
Jack Rosenthal, "The Age Boom," *New York Times Magazine*, 9 March
  1997, sec. 6, p. 42.
"The Lovebirds' Budget," *The Economist* 343, no. 8016 (10 May 1997): 16.
"Select Enemy. Delete," *The Economist* 342, no. 8007 (8 March 1997): 24.

Starting with a conjunction

Mary Cantwell, "Still at Work on a Self," *New York Times Magazine*, 9
  March 1997, sec. 6, p. 57.

Stephen S. Hall, "Genome Dread," *New York Times Magazine*, 18 January 1998, sec. 6, p. 12.

"The Need for Greed," *The Economist*, 339, no. 7964 (4 May 1996): 80.

Vladimir Nabokov, *Lectures on Literature* (1980; New York: Harcourt Brace Jovanovich, 1982), p. 4.

Semicolons

Jeffrey Goldberg, "Our Africa," *New York Times Magazine*, 2 March 1997, sec. 6, p. 77.

"Monarchs and Mountebanks," *The Economist* 345, no. 8048 (20 December 1997): 62.

"Capital Punishments," *The Economist* 345, no. 8048 (20 December 1997): 69.

Michiko Kakutani, "Taking Out the Trash," *New York Times Magazine*, 8 June 1997, sec. 6, p. 34.

Colon linking an example

"Lean Enough?" *The Economist* 338, no. 795d (10 February 1996): 59.

"The Birth of a New Species," in *Survey of the Software Industry* (insert), *The Economist* 339, no. 7967 (25 May 1996): 3.

Hubert B. Herring, "Diary," *New York Times*, 18 May 1997, sec. 4, p. 2.

John Tierney, "New York's Parallel Lives," *New York Times Magazine*, 19 October 1997, sec. 6, p. 51.

Colon linking an elaboration

"The Birth of a New Species," in *Survey of the Software Industry* (insert), *The Economist* 339, no. 7967 (25 May 1996): 5.

The Economist, "We Know You're Reading This," *The Economist* 338, no. 7952 (10 February 1996): 27.

Robert Hughes, "American Visions," *Time*, special issue May 1997, 9.

John Tierney, "Let's Give Peace a Chance," *New York Times Magazine*, 2 November 1997, sec. 6, p. 30.

Parallel constructions

"We Know You're Reading This," *The Economist* 338, no. 7952 (10 February 1996): 28.

The World Development Report 1997: The State in a Changing World (New York: Oxford University Press, 1997), p. 20.

Book Currents, *New Yorker Magazine* 73, no. 38 (8 December 1997): 3.

Vladimir Nabokov, *Lectures on Literature* (1980; New York: Harcourt Brace Jovanovich, 1982), p. 3.

The verb-free element

Kevin Barry, "Still Clueless," *New York Times Book Review*, 7 December 1997, sec. 7, p. 46.

"The Next Revolution," in *Survey: Business in Eastern Europe, The Economist* 345, no. 8044 (22 November 1997): 3.

Edwin Dobb, "Where the Good Begins," *Harper's* 297, no. 1778 (July 1998): 60.

Elizabeth Cady Stanton, quoted in *The Norton Anthology of Literature by Women*, ed. Sandra M. Gilbert and Susan Gubar, 2d ed. (New York: Norton, 1996), p. 465.

9. ONE-SYLLABLE OPENINGS

It

André Gide, quoted in *Bartlett's Familiar Quotations*, 16th ed. (Boston: Little Brown, 1968), p. 607.

Paul Krugman, "Does Getting Old Cost Society Too Much?" *New York Times Magazine*, 9 March 1997, sec. 6, p. 60.

Richard Wright, *12 Million Black Voices* (New York: Viking, 1941), p. 101.

Henry R. Luce, *The American Century* (New York: Farrar and Rinehart, 1941), p. 22.

There

Ken Auletta, "Redstones Secret Weapon," *New Yorker Magazine* 70, no. 45 (16 January 1995): 51.

Michael Parfit, "Breathless," *New York Times Book Review*, 7 December 1997, sec. 7, p. 24.

Ian Blecher, Letters to the Editor, *New Yorker Magazine* 71, no. 22 (31 July 1995): 9.

"The End of the Miracle?" *The Economist* 345, no. 8047 (13 December 1997): 19.

This

William Safire, "Day of Infamy," *New York Times Magazine*, 7 December 1997, sec. 6, p. 30.

"Panic in South Korea," *The Economist* 345, no. 8047 (13 December 1997): 16.

"The End of the Miracle?" *The Economist* 345, no. 8047 (13 December 1997): 18.

Carol Lloyd, "Cents and Sensibility," *New York Times Magazine,* 28 December 1997, sec. 6, p. 50.

That

"The Kyoto Compromise," *The Economist* 345, no. 8047 (13 December 1997): 16.

"Drop That Steak or We Shoot," *The Economist* 345, no. 8047 (13 December 1997): 15.

"The End of the Miracle?" *The Economist* 345, no. 8047 (13 December 1997): 18.

Holly Brubach, "Doc Rotella's Cure for the Thinking Athlete," *New York Times Magazine,* 2 November 1997, sec. 6, p. 49.

What

"All This, and a Korean Election Too," *The Economist* 345, no. 8047 (13 December 1997): 34.

David Handelman, "The Ambivalent-about-Prime-Time Players," *New York Times Magazine* 28 December 1997, sec. 6, p. 28.

William Safire, "The Incredible 'n' Credible," *New York Times Magazine,* 28 December 1997, sec. 6, p. 10.

Joseph Epstein, "Portraits by Max," *New Yorker Magazine* 73, no. 38 (8 December 1997): 108–10.

EXEMPLARY SENTENCES

Clive Crook, "Europe's Gamble," in *The World in 1998* (a publication of *The Economist*) pp. 11–32.

Michiko Kakutani, "Master of His Domain," *New York Times Magazine,* 1 February 1998, sec. 6, p. 20.

PART TWO

POWERFUL
PARAGRAPHS

AN APPROACH TO PARAGRAPHS   107
  Building paragraphs from a plan   108
  Getting off to a good start   108
  Summing up   111

1 UNIFY YOUR PARAGRAPHS AROUND
   STRONG POINTS   114
  Be clear about your subject   114
  Make a strong point   115
  Be sure every sentence bears on the point   116
  Repeat a key term   118
  Repeat a sentence structure—for sentences
    doing the same work   120
  Count the elements   122
  Signal what's to come   123
  Stick to one subject   124
  Stick to one verb form   126
  Fold two sentences into one   127

2 MAKE YOUR POINTS IN COMPELLING WAYS   130
   Lead with the point and support it   130
   Lead with the point and conclude with a
     comment   132
   Lead with the point and, using conjunctions,
     join details   133
   Lead with the point and list disparate details   134
   Lead with the point and follow it with a
     bulleted list   135
   Conclude with the point after introducing
     the subject   137
   Conclude with the point after listing
     disparate details   138
   Make the point in the middle   139
   Undermine a premise at the end of the
     paragraph   141
   Undermine a premise immediately   143
   Undermine a premise in the middle of the
     paragraph   144
   Start with a question and answer it immediately   145
   Start with a question and answer it in succeeding
     sentences   147
   Start with a question and answer it at the end   148
   Ask several questions and answer each
     immediately   149
   Imply the point in a series of details or examples   150
   Imply the point in a series of questions   151
   Imply the point by presenting two sides   153
   Imply the point in an analogy or syllogism   154

3 LINK YOUR PARAGRAPHS   156
   Repeat a word or phrase from the end
     of the preceding paragraph   156
   Turn the repeated word into a question   157
   Repeat an opening word or phrase   158
   Signal what's to come   159

Establish pairs across paragraphs 161
Ask a question at the end of one paragraph and
    answer it at the beginning of the next 162
Ask a question at the beginning of the second
    paragraph 163
Make a comment 165
Count 166
Place paragraphs in time 167
Announce an example 168
String examples together 169
Undermine 171

EXEMPLARY PARAGRAPHS 174

SOURCES 189

AN APPROACH TO PARAGRAPHS

MANY writers think of paragraphs as a collection of sentences framed by an indent and a carriage return, running perhaps ten or twelve lines. Few have the language to describe what's good—or bad—about a paragraph. This book shows you what it means for a paragraph to be unified, coherent, and well developed. The idea here is to give you a way of looking at paragraphs that will change the way you write.

A paragraph is unified if each sentence is clearly related to the point, coherent if you make it obvious to your reader how each sentence is linked to the point. You can make the link more obvious by repeating key words and phrases. You can also use transitional words and phrases to enumerate and coordinate a paragraph's sentences. And you can change the structure of your sentences to reveal parallel or subordinate ideas. These techniques do more than make your paragraphs coherent—they also give them pace.

A paragraph is well developed if its sentences unfold in a way that makes your argument perfectly clear to the reader. One of the best ways to do this is to express the point of the paragraph as a general statement in the first sentence and then to support it with details and examples in subsequent sentences. Used for perhaps half to two-thirds of all paragraphs in expository writing, this model is among the most common. Some of the other ways are to conclude with the point, to phrase the point as a question and answer, and to undermine an argument to make the opposite point. Still other ways include making a subtle (or not so subtle) comment at the end of a straightforward series of details. Deciding how you develop a paragraph generally depends on the details, examples, and comments you have to support your point.

BUILDING PARAGRAPHS FROM A PLAN

Strong paragraphs will emerge more easily if you have done some planning. (*Riveting Reports*, also in this series, is a good place to start.) A paragraph-by-paragraph plan helps you organize your material by going beyond an outline to identify the topic of each paragraph in an entire piece. You then write the topic of each paragraph at the top of a sheet of paper (or page screen, if you're online) and try to make a strong point about each topic. Finally you assemble your raw material—details, comments, examples—under those points. With your material thus organized, and your head significantly clearer, you're ready to write unified, coherent, well-developed paragraphs.

GETTING OFF TO A GOOD START

Opening paragraphs have tremendous effect on how—and whether—your piece will be read. The most common opening is the throat-clearing paragraph that blandly announces how the piece will unfold. What you want instead is to grab your readers' attention, rivet them to your message, and propel them through your argument. Here are a few ways to do just that.

Put your main message up front. Tell your readers exactly what you intend to get across to them by setting out your main and any supporting messages up front, where they can't be missed.

In no society today do women enjoy the same opportunities as men. This unequal status leaves considerable disparities between how much women contribute to human development and how little they share in its benefits.

Start with a gripping fact. Present a compelling (or even shocking) fact or statistic that you suspect your readers will find interesting.

Every twenty minutes or so, someone somewhere is killed or injured by a landmine. According to the United Nations more than 110m buried mines are left over from the 20th century's numerous wars—most of them in poor countries such as Afghanistan, Angola and Cambodia which can ill afford the cost of removing them.

Ask questions. Ask questions to draw your readers in as participants, enticing them to read on and find out the answers.

Swamped by voicemail and email? Prepare yourself for the next wave of digital communications deluge: instant messaging.

Set the scene. Descriptive details can pull readers in by helping them to visualize the scene you're setting.

Out here in Big Sky Country, high on a ridge in the Absaroka Range, a golden eagle soars, pushed upward by a stream of warm air. From its perch in a golden-leafed aspen, a Steller's jay the color of indigo shrieks at the interlopers 20 feet below.

A Clark's nutcracker drills into a pine cone, the only sound except the distant rumble from the Yellowstone River.

Surprise your readers. Humor can put your readers at ease, a tactic especially useful before launching into a controversial topic.

The bagpipe's appeal is difficult to explain. Playing it can be a lonely calling. At a party, nobody asks you to sit down and bang out a song. You wear a skirt. There are the jokes.

Present a brief history. Starting with a historical anecdote adds the interest of analogy—and boosts your credibility.

Even the early stages of the Industrial Revolution quickly made England the wealthiest society that had ever existed, but it took a long time for the wealth to be reflected in the earnings of ordinary workers. Economic historians still argue about whether real wages rose or fell between 1790 and 1830, but the very fact that there is an argument shows that the laboring classes did not really share in the nation's new prosperity.

It's happening again. As with early 19th century England, late 20th century America is a society being transformed by radical new technologies that have failed to produce a dramatic improvement in the lives of ordinary working families—indeed, these are the technologies whose introductions have been associated with stagnant or declining wages for many. The Industrial Revolution was not based on silicon and information; but in a deep sense the story is probably much the same.

Address your readers. Use the imperative to involve your readers personally.

Imagine it is late 1986 and you are managing a consumer electronics factory in Japan. Your business is in trouble. The deal struck at the Plaza Hotel the year before has doubled the value of the yen—the currency your manufacturing costs are based in—against the dollar, the currency of your biggest export market. Your workers are expensive and it is hard to find anyone to do jobs that involve the three ks—*kitamai, kiken, kitsui* (dirty, dangerous, or tough). The currencies of your most aggressive competitors, the Taiwanese and Koreans, have risen only slightly against the dollar and they are snatching market share away from you. What do you do?

Open with a quotation. Using someone else's well-put words can handily set the tone for what follows.

"Unsex me!" cried Lady Macbeth in a plea to the spirits that should probably be inscribed in the Pentagon somewhere.

"Character," says Aristotle, *"gives us qualities, but it is in actions—what we do—that we are happy or the reverse."* We have already decided that Aristotle is wrong and now we must face the consequences of disagreeing with him.

SUMMING UP

Powerful closing paragraphs convey the essence of an argument's main points without restating all of its detail. The strongest closing paragraphs put the main points in a broader perspective and provoke further thought.

Restate the essence of your main message. The most common kind of closing paragraph restates the conclusions of a report. Try to restate only the essence of your main messages, using new language or a new image.

There is a curve of time that separates Heman Sweatt and Cheryl Hopwood. It has been a long while since that spring afternoon in 1950 when, as a first-year Yale law student, I heard the promise of freedom in the voice of Thurgood Marshall. Since then, I have observed commendable progress, lately some tragic retrogression, and now I see even more clearly that, in the long, bloody history of the race relations in America, there is no more time for foolishness.

This example also pulls in the title of the report ("Achieving Analytical Wisdom"), linking the last line of the closing paragraph to the very beginning of the report. Readers will feel as though they have come full circle and will have a sense of completion.

Use a closing quotation. Sometimes someone else has already summed up the message of your piece quite well. If so, use it.

In the meantime, expatriates like Bowles and McPhillips cling stubbornly to their adopted city. "It still has this attraction, this inexplicable ability to pull at your heart and soul," McPhillips says. "There's the light, the air, the wind blowing through the strait, the interplay between Europe and Morocco that will never change. Tangier is indestructible."

This quotation offers proof of the writer's concluding idea:

Will the wily Mr. Castro change with the times? He seems to be incapable of it—incapable of abandoning his ideology even for the sake of increasing his chances of maintaining power. Fidel himself puts it this way. "It is the world that is changing. Cuba will not change . . . even death will not defeat us."

Pose a question. One question, or a series of questions, will suggest ways to branch from your argument or its possible trajectories. Or, as in this example, it can be used as a comment to linger in people's minds.

> The real differences between the mergers of the 1980s and previous waves do not lie either in the hostility of the bids or the nature of the financing. They lie in why the restructuring took place and in the forms of ownership and capital structure that were assumed to be superior to the old. As an Irish prime minister once said after listening to a long debate between his cabinet colleagues: "I understand how it works in practice. But how does it work in theory?"

Propose a challenge or future direction. Put your purpose into words by giving readers something concrete to do after reading your report.

> But the aim should be for the UN, through the Security Council, to decide where a UN-sponsored force should be deployed and have the capacity to man it, not to subcontract the job and the decision-making to individual members. Turning the UN into cheerleader, or belated picker-up of superpowers' problems, is not the way to improve peacekeeping. The UN's authority needs to be strengthened, not sidestepped.

At the end of Part Two, you'll find another sampling of paragraph models that can give your writing more variety and pace. Many of the techniques embodied in those models can bridge two paragraphs or develop an argument across a series of paragraphs. In between, you will learn how to identify the points of your paragraphs, how to present those points strongly, and how to support your points in clear, compelling ways to create powerful paragraphs.

1

UNIFY YOUR PARAGRAPHS AROUND STRONG POINTS

POINTLESS. That is one of the biggest problems a writer has with paragraphs: failing to tell readers the point of what they're reading. Close behind is having a point with no support: a succession of loose, even unrelated, sentences.

The solution to the first problem is simply to add a strong point—and to make it obvious, usually by leading with it. The solution to the second problem is to make sure that every sentence in a paragraph bears on the point—and then to clarify the supporting sentences by using the traditional rhetorical devices of repeating a key term, counting the elements, signaling what's to come, and changing the structure of sentences. These devices also make your paragraphs easier to read—and more likely to stay in your reader's mind.

BE CLEAR ABOUT YOUR SUBJECT

Writers rarely take the time to figure out the subject of a paragraph before they write one. But only by knowing the subject can you make a strong point about it. And only with a strong point can you assess whether all of a paragraph's sentences are related to it.

In the following paragraphs the subject is **boldfaced** and the point *italicized*. (In the first two sections of this book I have *italicized* what I surmise to be the point of many of the paragraphs.)

> **Manchuria** *openly displays its attachment to a bygone age.* In the port of Dalian, in Liaoning province, there is a Stalin Street; and in Shenyang, the province's capital, stands one of the few remaining public statues of Mao. In Harbin, the capital of Heilongjiang, a party official says that Mao's poems, set to music, are as suitable for karaoke sessions as "Love Story"; to prove it, he sings one.

> **Jeff Pulver** *is well and truly wired.* He is an Internet entrepreneur, with his fingers in many pipes, particularly the "fat pipe" that snakes into his home in Great Neck, New York. The fat pipe is a wire that can carry 1.5 bits of data a second. In lots of companies a pipe that fat is shared by hundreds of employees. Mr. Pulver has one all to himself. He thinks of it as rather expensive insurance against his Internet's principal curse: delay.

MAKE A STRONG POINT

Powerful paragraphs need more than obvious subjects—they need strong points. Usually stated explicitly at the start, sometimes implied, the point is a statement of opinion or fact, which you then support with the other sentences in your paragraph.

> *The growth of America's capital in recent years has indeed been remarkable.* The District of Columbia bar had fewer

than 1,000 members in 1950, now it has 61,000. The number of journalists in Washington soared from 1,500 to 12,000 over the same period. The staff of Congress has roughly doubled since 1979. On one estimate, 91,000 lobbyists of one sort or another grace the Washington area with their presence.

By almost any measure, *Chile in 1995 has an economy that it is difficult to find fault with.* Inflation is in single digits and declining. Foreign reserves at $14.8 billion are high and rising. The government consistently runs a healthy budget surplus. Exports grew by more than 25% last year. Foreign investment was $4.7 billion (9.1% of GDF). The unemployment rate, less than 6%, is one of the lowest in Latin America.

"Ulysses" has a long history of translation. It was greeted as a great work of literary modernism when it appeared in its highly original English in 1922. But it was available in German and French before it was legally for sale in Britain or the United States. Even the Latvians have their own version; the Japanese have four. Chinese translators never got around to it. After the Communist victory in 1949, such a work would have been dangerous.

BE SURE EVERY SENTENCE BEARS ON THE POINT

After you've written a paragraph, check to be sure each sentence supports the point. Too often, sentences are loosely related to the subject of the paragraph but not tied to the point.

In the following examples, the supporting sentences have been rated *yes* (Y) if clearly related, *no* (N) if unrelated, and *questionable* (?) if their relationship to the point is dubious.

Game theory, fathered 50 years ago by the great mathematician John von Neumann, *has become an important tool for economists and businesses.* Businesses apply it in sharpening their marketplace skills, drawing on available information, as a poker player does, to plot their next moves and guess the reaction of competitors. [Y] Economists use it in a broader sense to forecast interactions of all kinds. [Y] Strategists at Rand Corp. and elsewhere have applied it to anticipate the diplomatic and military moves of governments. [Y]

In the paragraph above, all the sentences clearly relate to the point. The pronoun *it* anchors *game theory* in each of the supporting sentences, which show how game theory has become an important tool.

Business is very bad at Porsche. Sales of the speedy luxury cars on which the company built its reputation have fallen by more than half in the space of just two years. [Y] The cars are known for their sporty design and superior performance. [N] The work force has been cut by 25 percent. [Y] Inside the plant workers are nervous and insecure. [?]

Sometimes unrelated sentences stick out grotesquely; others require scrutiny to ferret them out. In the preceding paragraph, the third sentence—on *sporty design*—sends the reader off course and diffuses the point. It should be cut. The fifth sentence may be true, but it would be more effective pulled into the fourth: "... *by 25 percent, leaving workers inside the plant nervous and insecure.*"

The life blood of a Chinese company is guanxi—*connections.* Penetrating layers of *guanxi* is like peeling an onion: first come connections between people with ancestors from the same province in China; then people from the same clan or village;

finally, the family. [Y] It does not matter much whether a
Chinese businessman is in Hong Kong or New York, he will always operate through *guanxi*. [Y] But these networks do not
enforce conformity. [?] Chinese tend to be far less concerned
with consensus than the Japanese. [N] As long as they honor
their word and look after their own, they can do whatever they
want. [N]

The second and third sentences clearly support the point—
that *connections* are *the life blood of a Chinese company*. The
fourth might be sliding into another point—and could open
another paragraph. The fifth and sixth sentences deal with this
second, albeit related point and undermine the paragraph's coherence.

REPEAT A KEY TERM

Once you've rid a paragraph of extraneous material, try repeating a key word or phrase to bind the sentences even more.
Many writers have an aversion to repetition, something they
generally acquire in the seventh grade. But using different terms
for the same idea simply to avoid repetition will confuse your
reader.

In this example, repeating the term *Mother's Day* ties the four
sentences together.

> *On Mother's Day this year MCI*, America's second-largest
> long-distance telephone company, *offered many of its domestic
> customers free calls*. Struck by an annual outbreak of filial sen-
> timent, Americans make more long-distance calls on *Mother's
> Day* than on any other day of the year. Americans also have
> almost a quarter of the world's telephone lines, so *Mother's*

Day traffic in the United States is probably the heaviest any-where in the world. Yet MCI felt it could offer a free service on *Mother's Day* without overloading its network.

The next version, by contrast, is loose—because it avoids rep-etition. The use of *that day* is fine in the second sentence, tying it to the first. But the third has no tie to *Mother's Day*, weaken-ing the attempted link of *this holiday* in the fourth.

On Mother's Day this year MCI, America's second-largest long-distance telephone company, *offered many of its domestic customers free calls.* Struck by an annual outbreak of filial sen-timent, Americans make more long-distance calls on that day than on any other day of the year. Americans also have almost a quarter of the world's telephone lines, so traffic in the United States is probably the heaviest anywhere in the world. Yet MCI felt it could offer a free service on this holiday without over-loading its network.

Repeating more than one word can create a resounding echo:

In Europe's first integration at the hands of bureaucratic Roman imperialists these quickening virtues had been stifled and therein lay the seeds of the empire's dissolution. Therein too lay the kernel of an oblique message for Gibbon's con-temporaries. And our contemporaries too?

The repetition of *therein* and *lay* ties the second sentence to the first, and the repetition of *too* and *contemporaries* ties the third to the second.

For 34 years he lived in the uneasy crucible of Congress, first tasting the frustrations of powerlessness and then exercising the prerogatives of power. He took his lessons through the haze of Camel cigarettes and over the bourbon and branch water that flowed in Sam Rayburn's secret hideaway. He took others from another master of leadership, Lyndon B. Johnson. Later, he dispensed lessons of his own, and sometimes they were lessons in brutal partisanship; his Republican rivals learned them not wisely but too well.

In the paragraph above, the subject of each sentence, *he*, ties all four sentences together. The repetition of *took* ties the third sentence to the second, and that of *lessons* ties the fourth.

REPEAT A SENTENCE STRUCTURE—FOR SENTENCES DOING THE SAME WORK

If sentences are doing similar work, they're easier to understand if they're similar in structure. As with repeating a key word or term, repeating a structure can strengthen the links among your supporting sentences and between those sentences and your point.

Here are some supportive sentences that open differently:

History has a capricious memory, and it's anyone's guess how it will remember James C. Wright Jr. of Texas. It may remember him grandly, because he was the House Speaker who most aggressively muscled his way into foreign policy. If he is remembered more simply, it will be as one of the forgotten figures who served between two white-haired partisans, Thomas P. O'Neill Jr. of Massachusetts and Newt Gingrich of Georgia. Or he may be poignantly remembered as the forlorn man who was toppled from the giddiest heights of American politics . . . over a book.

Not unreadable, but not nearly as unified or memorable as:

History has a capricious memory, and it's anyone's guess how it will remember James C. Wright Jr. of Texas. Perhaps grandly, as the House Speaker who most aggressively muscled his way into foreign policy. Perhaps simply, as one of the forgotten figures who served between two white-haired partisans, Thomas P. O'Neill Jr. of Massachusetts and Newt Gingrich of Georgia. Or perhaps poignantly, as the forlorn man who was toppled from the giddiest heights of American politics . . . over a book.

Here, repetition binds the three supporting sentences tightly, showing that each is a possibility. The repeated opening is especially effective for supporting sentences that could be arranged in (almost) any order, as with *grandly*, *simply*, and *poignantly*, though *poignantly* is the obvious finish.

Two more examples:

Crash. *Stockmarket bulls* can act as brave as they like but they *cannot deny the terror that this simple word strikes in their breasts.* They may reassure themselves with talk of record profits or the death of inflation. They may point out all the ways in which Wall Street's bull run is not like others which ended in tears. But they cannot deny the stark reality: stockmarkets are notoriously fickle and can turn against you at a moment's notice.

This book has three elements: *a description* of the terrible present state and future prospects of the American Economy, *a theory* of the causes of the dreadful condition, *and a prescription* for rescuing us. The description of our condition is grossly exaggerated. The theory of the causes of the alleged condition is inadequately supported. The prescription is, with some exceptions, unpersuasive.

COUNT THE ELEMENTS

If you have two or three discrete details to support your point, your readers may absorb them better if they are counted.

This paragraph does not count the supporting sentences:

The stance and style of the inaugurals seem to have gone through some different phases. The phase that lasted until Lincoln was that of the modest, classic public servant. William Howard Taft marked the end of the phase of the prosaic government executive. We are still in the phase of the assertive, theatrical leader-preacher. This classification is not waterproof. Theodore Roosevelt may belong in the theatrical leader-preacher phase and Warren G. Harding–Calvin Coolidge–Herbert Hoover in the prosaic government executive phase. But the trend is clear.

How many phases were there? Not clear. Note the difference that counting can make:

The stance and style of the inaugurals seem to have gone through three phases. The first, lasting until Lincoln, was that of the modest, classic public servant. The second, lasting through William Howard Taft, was of the prosaic government executive. The third, in which we are still, is the phase of the assertive, theatrical leader-preacher. This classification is not waterproof. Theodore Roosevelt may belong in the third phase and Warren G. Harding–Calvin Coolidge–Herbert Hoover in the second. But the trend is clear.

Here are two more examples of counting:

Two durable impressions of the past two decades: first, women have made considerable progress in a short time in building human capabilities; and second, women have gone a considerable distance towards gender equality in education and health. These impressions are cause for hope, not pessimism, in the future.

Digitalization implies three things. First, that music can be faithfully recorded on a durable medium. That part has already happened, and saved the music business without changing it much. Second, that such recordings can be compressed and distributed in new ways. That is just beginning in America. Third, it implies that computers can speak the language of music.

SIGNAL WHAT'S TO COME

Revealing the relationships between sentences, transitional words can signal continuation *(and, further, furthermore, in addition, similarly)*, reversal *(or, but, still, despite, otherwise, even so, nevertheless)*, and conclusion *(so, thus, after all, in sum, in short, in brief)*.

Here's a paragraph with no signals:

One of Mr. Blair's reasons for linking Britain and 2000 so closely is surely off the mark; strictly, the day begins at Greenwich, because it is at zero degrees of longitude, the meridian from which hours forward or back are conventionally reckoned. It is argued, the millennium will start in Britain. Tell that to the Russians, or to any of the majority of mankind that lives eastwards of Greenwich up to the International Date Line and whose midnight comes well before Britain's.

The paragraph makes sense, but the jump from the first sentence to the second is jarring and the remaining sentences are loose. Consider the following alternative, with signals:

Yet one of Mr. Blair's reasons for linking Britain with 2000 so closely is surely off the mark: strictly, the day begins at Greenwich, because it is at zero degrees of longitude, the meridian from which hours forward or back are conventionally reckoned. So, it is argued, the millennium will start in Britain. But tell that to the Russians, or indeed to any of the majority of mankind that lives eastwards of Greenwich up to the International Date Line and whose midnight comes well before Britain's.

Here are two more examples of deftly signaling what's to come:

Despite its one-sided arguments and hyperbolic claims, *The Great Betrayal* ought to stir discussion of such alternatives to the free-market internationalist status quo. Contrary to the best hopes of its advocates, the status quo has not extinguished the flames of nationalism but may actually be feeding them. If more of Buchanan's critics don't realize this soon, they may, ironically, end up leaving the stage to Buchanan himself.

This commercial dominance has been protected by a 10,000-strong private army, which has long fought off efforts by the central government in Yangon to bring it under control. As a result, Khun Sa is a rich man, with a lucrative market position to protect. So when, on New Year's Day, government troops walked unopposed into his headquarters at Ho Mong, it looked less like a military defeat, more as if the drug peddler had cut one more deal.

STICK TO ONE SUBJECT

If all the sentences in a paragraph are about one person, one idea, one country, try using the same noun or pronoun as the subject of each sentence.

Here is a paragraph with a new subject for each sentence:

In 1956 Endicott Peabody stood for election as attorney general of Massachusetts. Victory was not his. Next was a (failed) run at the Democratic nomination for the governorship of the state. Then the United States Senate candidacy—another loss. Hence the move to New Hampshire, with unsuccessful attempts for both houses of Congress. Endicott Peabody's record of honourable failure was briefly interrupted in 1962 when, after a lengthy recount of the votes, he was elected governor of Massachusetts. But two years later defeat was again the victor.

Compare that with *Endicott Peabody* as the subject for all sentences but one:

In 1956 Endicott Peabody stood for election as attorney general of Massachusetts. He lost. In 1958 he stood again, and again lost. In 1960 he sought the Democratic nomination for the governorship of the state, and failed. In 1966 he was a candidate for the United States Senate, and lost. In the 1980s he moved to New Hampshire and tried for both houses of Congress, but, sadly, lost again. Endicott Peabody's record of honourable failure was briefly interrupted in 1962 when, after a lengthy recount of the votes, he was elected governor of Massachusetts. But two years later he was defeated.

The new subject of the next-to-the-last sentence works because it signals Peabody's sole victory.

Two more examples:

Unbiased outsiders might blame languages, bad products and state intervention. (Britain's music and publishing industries, not hampered in these ways, compete head-to-head with

America's.) They might admit that Hollywood's libraries and worldwide distribution system give it a head start. But they would also note that when Europe produces films intended to please audiences as well as critics ("Four Weddings and a Funeral", for instance) it can do surprisingly well. And they would note too (as many in Hollywood do) that Tinseltown's bloated costs leave it surprisingly vulnerable to commercial competition. None of these thoughts has occurred to the lunatics running the EU's art asylum.

Gertrude Stein was not the stereotypical poor and alienated intellectual who was an enemy of capitalism. She always had a comfortable income, derived from her inheritance and supplemented after she turned 60 by her publishing royalties. She also had great investments—in Picassos, Matisses, and other paintings. Far from being alienated, she was the internationally recognized grande dame of a group of rising geniuses. And she was not an intellectual, having little interest in general ideas about economics or politics. "The real ideas," she said, "are not the relation of human beings as groups but a human being to himself inside him and that is an idea that is more interesting than humanity in groups."

Note how both paragraphs join equally weighted supporting sentences with *also* and *and*.

STICK TO ONE VERB FORM

Using one verb form rather than unnecessarily jumping from one form to another is always a good way to unify a paragraph.

The first paragraph uses a variety of verb forms, the second, only one.

Despite their stony homes, corals are fragile creatures. They will be crushed if you press too hard on them. If you cover them with silt, they can no longer feed on small passing animals. Blotting out the light by promoting the growth of algae in the waters above them would cause the other algae, with which they live symbiotically, to lose their ability to photosynthesize.

Despite their stony homes, corals are fragile creatures. Press too hard on them and they will be crushed. Cover them with silt and they can no longer feed on small passing animals. Blot out the light by promoting the growth of algae in the waters above them and other algae, with which they live symbiotically, can no longer photosynthesize.

The three imperatives of the second paragraph unify the three ideas loosely connected in the first.

In the next paragraph, the sentences are also similar in structure.

Ours cannot come out of the vision of any one man. It must be the product of the imaginations of many men. It must be a sharing with all peoples of our Bill of Rights, our Declaration of Independence, our Constitution, our magnificent industrial products, our technical skills. It must be an internationalism of the people, by the people and for the people.

FOLD TWO SENTENCES INTO ONE

Whenever two short sentences have the same subject, see whether you can fold one into the other—to show your reader which is the less important idea, which the more. Such folding is one of the easiest and most effective ways of picking up the pace of your paragraphs and tightening your sentences.

Compare this:

Seven Japanese trust banks have "volunteered" to reduce the purchase of foreign securities by their pension funds. They have done this on orders from the ministry of finance.

with this:

Seven Japanese trust banks, on orders from the ministry of finance, have "volunteered" to reduce the purchase of foreign securities by their pension funds.

This:

These pension funds have been investing abroad more than 30% of their net intake of funds during the past seven months. They have been tempted by high interest rates and Wall Street's bull run.

with this:

Tempted by high interest rates and Wall Street's bull run, these pension funds have been investing abroad more than 30% of their net intake of funds during the past seven months.

And this:

Now they will cut overseas investment to 20%. They hope to reduce capital outflows and so to strengthen the yen.

with this:

> Now they will cut overseas investment to 20%, hoping to re-
> duce capital outflows and so to strengthen the yen.

For each of these three pairs of sentences, the writer subordi-
nated the less important idea to the more important by combin-
ing both in one sentence.

2

MAKE YOUR POINTS IN COMPELLING WAYS

FEW writers consider how or where to make a point in a paragraph. Most express the point in the first sentence and support it in subsequent sentences with details and examples. While effective, this construction becomes less so when it is overused, and more so when alternated with other ways of making a point. Deciding how to make your point depends on the details, examples, and comments you have to support it.

LEAD WITH THE POINT AND SUPPORT IT

The most common way to develop a paragraph is to state the point in the first sentence and support it, in subsequent sentences, with evidence: details, examples, and comments. When you lead with the point, your reader can identify it immediately, and a skimmer can pick up your line of argument by reading the first sentence of each paragraph. This form of development is what most of us use for two-thirds of our writing.

Motorists can be a lonely lot. They may get periodic traffic updates along with the news, chat and music from their car radios. With cell phones, they can even talk back to the outside world—asking for directions and apologising for being late. But, by and large, drivers are cut off more than most people from the torrent of information that pervades modern life. And it's a good thing, too, some might say.

After the point about secular trends, the second sentence identifies one trend and the third elaborates on it, while the fourth identifies another trend and the fifth, sixth, and seventh elaborate on it.

Here are two more paragraphs with leading points that are clearly supported in the sentences that follow them:

As big trees go, the baobab, Adansonia digitata, *is a whopper.* While it doesn't have the majestic height of North America's sequoia or the serpentine grandeur of Africa's red-leaved ficus, it has, well, presence. In fact, South Africa's bushmen believe the tree, some time after its creation, offended the gods, who then commanded it to grow upside down. And in the winter dry season, when the baobab loses its leaves, that's what it looks like—a massive, squat succulent, with its roots sticking up in the air.

In America, the second most important cause of increased income inequality has been a change in household structure. In the 1950s most households consisted of two parents, only one of whom was a wage-earner. Now society is more polarized between two-earner households and jobless single parent families. It is hard for single mothers to earn good incomes. The proportion of families headed by women among the poorest fifth of households has doubled over the past 40 years to around 35%. In contrast, the richest fifth of households is increasingly dominated by high-income two-earner couples: well-paid women tend to marry rich men.

LEAD WITH THE POINT AND CONCLUDE WITH A COMMENT

Concluding a paragraph with a comment can inject a bit of your personality and, at times, humor. Comments can also put a paragraph in perspective, create a bridge to the next paragraph, or reinforce your point after presenting a series of facts.

Geography is not geology, but they can be interlinked in surprising ways. Geographically, Sakhalin Island is part of the Russian Far East, though half of it was Japanese territory until 1945. Geologically, though, it is a northward extension of Japan and thus prone to the same sort of seismic ups and downs as the rest of that archipelago. Earthquakes are no respectors of political boundaries.

Globally, the increasing stature of humans has untold environmental consequences. Everyone knows that we need more energy and natural resources to meet the needs of the earth's population as it grows. But virtually no one thinks about the increasing needs of people who are growing taller and heavier. Larger human size is directly related to increased energy consumption. The hot water needs of the average household, for example, are a function of size; hot water needs for showers are body-surface-area related, baths are body-volume related. So a population of larger people puts increased demands on hot water heaters.

Try inserting a comment as a stand-alone fragment:

If Japan's banks dumped their bonds, long-term rates might rise, but short-term ones would fall. No catastrophe, that.

as part of a sentence:

> *Mice whose RNA could not be edited developed epileptic seizures and died:* a heavy penalty for taking no notice of the editor.

or as a single word:

> Slyly, *they give "representational painting" an entirely new meaning.*

Gauge how much humor, irreverence, and personal opinion your readers will tolerate: don't make so many comments that they distract readers from your argument.

LEAD WITH THE POINT AND, USING CONJUNCTIONS, JOIN DETAILS

If you have, say, three supporting sentences of equal weight (none more important than the others), try linking them with *also* and *and* in the pattern shown here: X *is* . . . , X *is also* . . . , *and* X *is* . . . . By using these conjunctions and the same pronoun in each sentence, you can stress the equality or sequence of the details, pulling your readers through the paragraph.

> *At first sight the virtues of teamwork look obvious.* Teams make workers happier by giving them the feeling that they are shaping their own jobs. They also increase efficiency by eliminating layers of managers whose job was once to pass orders downwards. And, in principle, they enable a company to draw on the skills and imagination of a whole workforce, instead of relying on a specialist to watch out for mistakes and suggest improvements.

Germany is generous to immigrants. For a start, and in deference to their bloodline, it receives each year more than 200,000 Russians, the *Aussiedler* (outsettlers) whose German ancestors moved to Russia two centuries ago. On moral grounds, it takes in any Russian Jews who want to come. It has also admitted (in theory temporarily, though it may turn out permanently) more than half the entire outflow of refugees from the wars in the Balkans. And until three years ago, when it tightened its wide-open asylum laws, it received a good three-quarters of all third-world asylum-seekers reaching the European Union. Beyond that, it is home to some 2m Turkish immigrants originally taken in as "guest workers."

Note how this pattern strings the details together, injecting pace. The starting point is to look for details that start with—or could start with—the same subject and that appear to be of roughly equal importance. It works best if you have three details.

LEAD WITH THE POINT AND LIST DISPARATE DETAILS

Sometimes you can leave out such supporting conjunctions as *also* and *and* to add an edgy cadence to your details. Without conjunctions the series hits the reader in quick bursts, making each detail stand out. It also gives the impression that the list is not exhaustive.

Sierra Leone's post-dictatorship problems are almost absurd in their breadth. It once exported rice; now it can't feed itself. The life span of the average citizen is 39, the shortest in Africa. Unemployment stands at 87 percent and tuberculosis is spreading out of control. Corruption, brazen and ubiquitous, is a cancer on the economy.

Here the writer even leaves out the conjunction between the clauses of the first supporting sentence, joining them instead with a semicolon: *It once exported rice; now it can't feed itself.* Notice, too, how a consistent verb, *is*, binds the sentences of the paragraph.

Below, short sentences are even more staccato:

> *After a French winter of discontent, comes a hint of spring.* The economy is starting to pick up. The seemingly inexorable rise in unemployment is slowing. Taxes, having reached a record high, are at last dropping. Interest rates are at their lowest level in 35 years. Trade is booming. Business morale is less flat. Even President Jacques Chirac and Alain Juppé, his Gaullist prime minister, are finally edging their way up from their previous abysmal depths in the opinion polls.

Supporting sentences made up of disparate details have different subjects. Since you are stripping the paragraph of its linking conjunctions, use all present-tense verbs or even the same verb to enhance cohesion. (For more on parallel structure, see "Stick to one subject," page 124, and "Stick to one verb form," page 126.) To try it, start with more than two details of equal weight. Short details work best. Pile them up. See what happens.

LEAD WITH THE POINT AND FOLLOW IT WITH A BULLETED LIST

A list of numerical facts, complicated details, or recommendations can be difficult for readers to lift off the page from a block of text. Breaking that block into bulleted items clarifies those elements and works well for setting up a line of argument.

Why do this?

- To articulate three, four, or more facts
- To relieve a dense block of text or a long series
- To set each element apart, making it easier to remember
- To highlight a list of recommendations or important ideas

The ratio of global trade to GDP has been rising over the past decade, but it has been falling for 44 developing countries, with more than a billion people. *The least developed countries*, with 10% of the world's people, *have only 0.3% of world trade*—half their share of two decades ago.

The list goes on:

- More than half of all developing countries have been bypassed by foreign direct investment, two-thirds of which has gone to only eight developing countries.
- Real commodity prices in the 1990s were 45% lower than those in the 1980s—and 10% lower than the lowest level during the Great Depression, reached in 1932.
- The terms of trade for the least developed countries have declined a cumulative 50% over the past 25 years.
- Average tariffs on industry country imports from the least developed countries are 30% higher than the global average.
- Developing countries lose about $60 billion a year from agricultural subsidies and barriers to textile exports in industrial nations.

If financial systems are to reach low-income female entrepreneurs and producers, delivery systems need to respond to the common characteristics of low-income women and their businesses:

- Women have less experience in dealing with formal financial institutions.
- Women tend to have smaller enterprises and fewer assets.
- Women are less likely to own land or other assets and face legal barriers to borrowing in many countries.

- Illiteracy rates are higher among women.
- Low-income women tend to concentrate on different economic activities than low-income men.

The trick to writing this kind of paragraph is knowing when *not* to do it. Some reports have bullets everywhere. Used too frequently, they lose their effectiveness and become an excuse for not writing complete paragraphs. That said, there are good reasons for using them: to organize many numerical facts or to emphasize important recommendations.

CONCLUDE WITH THE POINT AFTER INTRODUCING THE SUBJECT

Occasionally, put the point at the end of a paragraph to build suspense. Do this sparingly, however, because readers tire of having to wait for you to get to the point.

One way to conclude with the point: introduce a subject, discuss it, then make a point about it at the end.

For as long as humans have co-operated in meeting their material needs, they have been falling out over who gets what. Quarrels over distribution have always been part of the background noise of politics. Sometimes they have been much more than that. At certain points they have mounted in intensity and provoked a crisis, later subsiding as they were resolved or otherwise forgotten. The turning points in this cycle have marked some of the most traumatic events of human history. *If concerns over economic inequality are mounting once again, it is a matter of more than passing interest.*

Imagine that a mad scientist went back to 1950 and offered to transport the median family to the wondrous world of the

1990s, and to place them at, say, the 25th percentile level. The 25th percentile of 1996 is a clear material improvement over the median of 1950. Would they accept his offer? Almost surely not—because in 1950 they were middle class, while in 1996 they would be poor, even if they lived better in material terms. *People don't just care about their absolute material level, they care about their level compared with others.*

Although it may be tempting, resist the urge to impose this design on perfectly sound leading-point paragraphs just to add rhetorical interest. One good place to use a concluding-point paragraph is at the start of a piece. In this prime location, concluding-point paragraphs lead readers into a piece gently.

Another place to use this pattern is when you're trying to make a point that you know might be hard for your readers to swallow. By putting the point at the end, you allow time for a softening preface and give yourself a chance to explain your position.

CONCLUDE WITH THE POINT AFTER LISTING DISPARATE DETAILS

Another way to conclude with the point is to list disparate details and bring them together with a point at the end. The short bursts pile up somewhat mysteriously until the point, even the subject, is revealed at the end.

Black helicopters hover menacingly over Michigan; trains loaded with white UN trucks trundle across Oregon. Sinister? You bet: the onset of world government, no less. Or rather a sample of the nonsense that lands daily on a congressman's desk. After a bit, the congressman pays attention. He knows that the helicopters were American, flying low-level training missions; that the trucks were Canadian, destined for a UN

mission; that the people who propagate this sort of stuff are nuts. *But behind the tall stories is something serious: the intense mistrust that some Americans feel for almost anything the UN does.*

You can see America wilting in downtown Silver Spring. Old office blocks stand empty. A grand art deco cinema is frequented only by ghosts. Glitzy department stores have decamped to out-of-town shopping malls. Tattoo parlours, pawnbrokers, discounters remain. This decay, multiplied a thousand times in towns across America, is especially painful in a country built on the idea of progress. Lacking a common history, ethnicity, or even language, *Americans are held together by a singular optimism: by the American dream.*

Too colorful for some pieces, obviously inappropriate for others, this pattern can puzzle your readers, so be sure the details are vivid enough to intrigue them. If readers don't make it to the end of the paragraph, they will not get to your point.

Writing this kind of paragraph can take practice. If you have a series of powerful, descriptive details, try stringing them together. If you like the results but the effect is dubious, you might want to make the point at the beginning (see "Lead with the point and list disparate details," page 134).

The other thing to consider is your subject. This structure often works well for controversial points because as the details unfold, your readers become curious and follow along in the deduction.

MAKE THE POINT IN THE MIDDLE

Sometimes, though not often, your point is best put in the middle of the paragraph. The first few sentences of the paragraph introduce the (perhaps surprising) point and soften its arrival.

Amber is fossil resin, the consequence of tree injuries suffered millions of years ago. Its early significance to science can be seen from its ancient Greek name—elektron. Until the invention of batteries, rubbing amber was the best-known way of generating (static) electricity. *But amber's modern importance to science is as a trap.* Hundreds of species of ancient creepy-crawly are known to paleontologists only because they blundered into a blob of resin many million years ago. David Grimaldi, a curator whose fascination with amber led to the museum's global search for exhibits and treasures, says that amber's paleontological role is much misunderstood, thanks largely to its appearance in "Jurassic Park."

In the paragraph above, the first three sentences inform readers about amber's historical importance, which sets up a comparison with amber's significance today.

The first few sentences of the paragraph below establish the writer's position and provide background to the point:

Among the many convenient targets that Republican politicians and intellectuals have at their disposal, the one at which they direct their fire with perhaps the most delight is the academy. George Will, William Bennett, and other right-wing thinkers never tire of recounting the follies of professors and of portraying them as naive, duped, and possibly duplicitous. *The right has made especially clever and effective use of the widespread suspicion of multiculturalism.* A large portion of the American middle class has been made to believe that the universities are under the control of a "political correctness" police. This false belief has made it easier for the racists, the sexists, and the homophobes to dismiss their opponents as far-out, self-intoxicated radicals—out of touch with the sound common sense of mainstream America.

To build this kind of paragraph, try folding a paragraph with a strong point into a more general opening or introductory paragraph. Remember that you are placing an important sentence in the least conspicuous place, so be sure that the point is strong enough to stand out—even if you're trying to soften it.

UNDERMINE A PREMISE AT THE END OF THE PARAGRAPH

Undermining an idea is a clever way to make your point stand out while taking the claws out of an opposing view. The decision about undermining at the beginning, middle, or end of a paragraph depends on how much information you want to give in support of the premise.

Undermining at the end of a paragraph is like concluding with the point—but in a backhanded way. It shows your understanding of an alternative point of view—then slams the direction of the argument into reverse.

Undermining can:

• highlight an opponent's flaws or weaknesses
• present (and refute) a common misconception
• introduce tension or create the atmosphere of debate.

It is widely believed, especially by labor union officials, that the fall of the blue collar industrial worker in the developed countries was largely, if not entirely, caused by moving production "offshore" to countries with abundant supplies of unskilled labor and low wage rates. *But this is not true.*

In the above example, your readers have an immediate clue that you don't agree with the premise *(It is widely believed)*. The strong statement at the end *(But this is not true)* leaves no doubt about your position, presumably to be elaborated in the following paragraph.

Here is another paragraph that undermines the opening point at the end:

Whenever an attempt is made to marry economics with Charles Darwin, it is well to raise a sceptical eyebrow. And the case for scepticism is all the stronger when natural selection is invoked to explain some pattern of things which, pretty clearly, could be changed by a simple act of will. For many years it has been argued that the present shape of the American corporation, in which a vast and dispersed group of shareholders exercises little or no control over the firm's managers, is in some way preordained. Organising firms like this, runs the argument, is simply the most efficient way of adapting to the demands of modern capitalism. *This view has its alluring points, but is wrong.*

Think of a premise you disagree with, opening it with a phrase like:

- *It is widely believed*
- *Many people think*
- *It may seem*
- *At first glance*

Then give the reader a few details about the premise, details that you can later turn to your advantage as you support your points. Along the way, you might intersperse such phrases as "it is argued" and "so goes the argument," to remind readers that you are not presenting your own view. Last, shift the direction of the argument by undermining the premise, perhaps signaling the shift with:

- *Yet*
- *But*
- *Actually*
- A *closer look reveals*
- *On the contrary*

UNDERMINE A PREMISE IMMEDIATELY

Sometimes, you may not need to elaborate on the premise you intend to debunk, allowing you to attack it immediately.

> But capital gains are special, the engines of entrepreneurship and growth. No. *There is nothing special about capital gains.* Simple accounting alchemy can turn almost any form of income into a capital gain, and will do so if the tax rate is different enough. Capital gains are often—but not always—the reward for risk taking, whereas dividends and interest are usually the payoff of safer investments. And risk taking is swell. But the market will reward a higher risk with a higher payoff—if the risk makes sense, and if you believe in the market.

> The point is well taken; *it is also misleading.* The issue is not the difficulty of writing but the fetishizing of difficulty, the belief that fractured English, name dropping, and abstractions guarantee profundity, professionalization, and subversion. With this belief comes the counter-belief: lucidity implies banality, amateurism, capitalism, and conservatism.

Undermining immediately is more abrupt than undermining at the end. Its quick shift can also be used as a transition between paragraphs (see "Link your paragraphs," pages 156–173).

UNDERMINE A PREMISE IN THE MIDDLE OF THE PARAGRAPH

Undermining a premise after you've given readers some background allows you to fit the whole process (state premise, support it, undermine it with a point, support point) into one paragraph. That, however, can make for long paragraphs.

> Chroniclers of the rise of the industrial worker tend to highlight the violent episodes—especially the clashes between strikers and the police, as in America's Pullman strike. The reason is probably that the theoreticians and propagandists of socialism, anarchism, and communism—beginning with Marx and continuing to Herbert Marcuse in the 1960s—incessantly wrote and talked of "revolution" and "violence." *Actually, the rise of the industrial worker was remarkably nonviolent.* The enormous violence of this century—the world wars, ethnic cleansings, and so on—was all violence from above rather than violence from below; and it was unconnected with the transformation of society, whether the dwindling of farmers, the disappearance of domestic servants, or the rise of the industrial worker. In fact, no one even tries anymore to explain these great convulsions as part of the "crisis of capitalism," as was standard Marxist rhetoric only thirty years ago.

> At first glance, it may seem absurd to propose that the cash visible in the capital is symptomatic of things getting better elsewhere across Russia. During the past four years industrial production has halved (America's fell by less than a third dur-

ing the Depression). *Government data, however, give cause for guarded optimism.* The decline in industrial output may have bottomed out; output has been steady for the past three months; living standards have actually improved. According to Goskomstat, the official collector of statistics, real (i.e., adjusted for inflation) household incomes rose by 18% in the year to July, and real household consumption by 10%. There are also signs of changes in the pattern of consumption: imports of chicken and red meat rose from 90,000 tonnes in January to 399,000 tonnes in August. Critics of reform will complain that Russia cannot afford to live on imported food — yet, in the first eight months of this year, Russia had a trade surplus of 11.7 billion.

To break these paragraphs up, you could put all the supporting sentences into a separate paragraph.

START WITH A QUESTION AND ANSWER IT IMMEDIATELY

Asking a question in the first line of a paragraph grabs readers' attention and sets up your point. Using an immediate, direct answer to make your point demonstrates a firm stance, emphasized by the confidence of a fragment.

Perhaps heightism is just a western cultural prejudice? *Sadly not.* In Chinese surveys, young women always rate stature high among qualifications for a future mate. Indeed, the prejudice appears to be universal.

So will squash eventually rival tennis as a spectator sport, and will Jansher Khan and Peter Marshall become as rich and famous as Pete Sampras and Andre Agassi? *Almost certainly not.*

For all the gimmicks of a glasswalled court, a special white ball and more and better cameras, squash remains fearsomely difficult to televise. Not only does the ball move too fast but the camera lens foreshortens the action. Squash, therefore, is destined to remain a sport better played than watched. Given its propensity for what the tennis authorities term "audible obscenities", that may be just as well.

Immediate answers make you seem—merely seem—unequivocal. They also engage your readers with a conversational tone. And they don't leave the answer to the reader.

An indirect answer is less firm. In the next paragraph, the writer avoids offending anybody by slithering:

Can the euro still be stopped? In Germany, both a driving force behind a single European currency and home to the biggest contingent of sceptics, a last-minute bid to delay its introduction has drawn ridicule from the government. "I am as sure [the euro] will be launched as I am of hearing 'Amen' in church," said the foreign minister, Klaus Kinkel. Maybe, if he does not get caught in the traffic that is building up alarmingly en route.

The next paragraph also ends with a question, throwing the first point into doubt and providing a transition to the paragraph that follows it:

Why is Dylan [Thomas's] legacy so ambivalent? *His reputation for being a drunk sits uneasily amid the Methodist chapels of South Wales.* When Dylan's Bookshop opened in the town 25 years ago, old men would come in, stare at the first editions and other memorabilia, and exclaim: "I knew him, the bloody waster." But was it entirely true?

Whether answered directly or indirectly, questions bring your readers closer to the text by making them feel part of the discourse. Compare this point:

> Our current system of teaching and learning is not very effective.

with this one:

> How effective is our current system of teaching and learning? Not very.

A question and immediate answer can thus make a flat point more arresting.

START WITH A QUESTION AND ANSWER IT IN SUCCEEDING SENTENCES

If the question defies a simple, straightforward answer, answer it in several sentences. You will still grab your audience's attention with an opening question but will reveal the answer more slowly.

This form works well for setting up a complicated or involved point, or for suggesting a point without stating it directly.

> So *why is the countryside booming?* Agricultural growth accelerated in the 1980s; roads and electricity reached most villages in the 1980s, helping start new businesses in transport and construction as well as manufacturing. The spread of electricity has raised productivity in the countryside, as well as increasing rural demand for electrically driven gadgets. As electricity has spread television, so television has presented India's villagers with the joys of the consuming life.

So *how can you tell if a Halls cough drop is too old?* After two years, the cough drop begins to look cloudy, it becomes softer and stickier, loses shape and begins to "flow into the cracks and crevices" of its wrapper, a Warner-Lambert spokesman says. Though the drops essentially contain the properties of hard candy, the company says the lozenges lose their effectiveness after about two and a half years.

In both paragraphs, the opening questions give the reader a lens for focusing on the sentences that follow.

START WITH A QUESTION AND ANSWER IT AT THE END

When you want to explore several possibilities or give reasons before answering a question, try putting the answer at the end of the paragraph. The effect is to make you seem thoughtful, thorough, cautious.

This kind of paragraph is similar to one that concludes with the point after introducing the subject (page 137). And here, too, be sure you don't lose your reader before arriving at your point—in this case, the answer to the opening question.

How many ideas—and how much fact—can a novel contain before it begins to turn into something else altogether—a work of non-fiction, for instance? Some famous examples spring to mind. The Napoleonic armies marched right the way through Tolstoy's epic "War and Peace" without protest from the author. One of the 18th century's best works of fiction, Laurence Sterne's "Tristram Shandy," was also one of the oddest novels ever written—part eccentric autobiography and part an examination of the nature of time. Closer to our own day, Norman Mailer fashioned his greatest novel, "The Executioner's Song," from the gruesome lineaments of a mass-murderer called Gary Gilmore. So how much can a novelist get away with? *It entirely depends upon whether or not he can sustain our interest by sheer force of persuasive imaginative skill.*

Why did the highly paid economists in the investment banks and the international financial institutions fail to predict the crisis? The IMF did issue several warnings to Thailand during the year before the collapse, but the government ignored it. *The handful of economists who rang alarm bells,* such as Jim Walker at Crédit Lyonnais and Mark McFarland at Peregrine Securities, *were generally thought to be too gloomy.*

In the first paragraph, the writer sets out three examples, restates the question, and then gives the answer to make the paragraph's point. In the second paragraph, the writer gives one answer immediately, undermines it, and concludes with the point, nicely sandwiching the supportive details.

ASK SEVERAL QUESTIONS AND ANSWER EACH IMMEDIATELY

A series of answered questions can give a paragraph a bantering, argumentative tone. And if you know your readers are going to have questions about the point you are making, try asking the questions yourself so that you can address each of them directly.

But which countries should represent these regions. India? Pakistan says no. Brazil? Argentina says no. Nigeria? Everybody says no. *Solutions galore have been suggested:* rotating members, tenured members, first-, second- and third-rank members, members without veto power, dropping the veto altogether or promising to use it in exceptional circumstances only.

You may say that the wretched of the earth should not be forced to serve as hewers of wood, drawers of water, and sewers of sneakers for the affluent. But what is the alternative? Should they be helped with foreign aid? Maybe—although the historical record of regions like southern Italy suggest that such aid has a tendency to promote perpetual dependence. Anyway, there isn't the slightest prospect of significant aid materializing. Should their own governments provide more social justice? Of course—but they won't, or at least, not because we tell them to. And as long as you have no realistic alternative to industrialization based on low wages, *to oppose it means that you are willing to deny desperately poor people the best chance they have of progress for the sake of what amounts to an aesthetic standard*—that is, the fact that you don't like the idea of workers being paid a pittance to supply rich Westerners with fashion items.

In the first paragraph, the writer uses questions to bring up and shoot down three possibilities, conveying the difficulties of reaching a consensus. In the second paragraph, the writer uses questions to open a conversation.

IMPLY THE POINT IN A SERIES OF DETAILS OR EXAMPLES

Most writers imply too many of their points—which their readers, bewildered, fail to infer. But having one point-led paragraph after another can get monotonous. So, when it's really possible to get a point across without stating it, give your reader some relief—and credit for being able to figure things out.

For one thing, Milan is shrinking—the population has fallen from 1.6m in 1981 to 1.3m today. The economy, which boomed in the 1980s, is dozier. Unemployment, now 8%, has been rising. In 1994–95, the number of businesses rose by only 2%, compared with 35% for Italy as a whole. Although Milan is home to five good universities and has far more head offices of multinationals than any other city in Italy, it is struggling to attract new blood. Even in areas of traditional strength—fashion, banking, publishing, advertising and high technology—Milan is losing its grip. Buildings once started seem to remain unfinished for ever. Prostitution is spreading.

Point: Milan is losing its power economically and intellectually.

[Meteorite] specimens prized for their beauty or rare composition can sell for more than $500 a gram (barely one twenty-eighth of an ounce), while meteorites from Mars, only 12 of which are known to have been recovered, go for more than $1,000 a gram. Mr. Killgore's daily harvest on a recent trip to the Chilean desert was $2,000 in meteorite nuggets.

Point: Meteorite specimens are rising in value.

This kind of paragraph needs strong details to hold it up. The point should begin to be obvious in the first or second detail and should be confirmed by the rest—don't keep your reader guessing.

If the details cannot stand on their own, you can easily make the point explicit and put it at the beginning or the end.

IMPLY THE POINT IN A SERIES OF QUESTIONS

Turning everything into a question emphasizes the unknown elements of an issue and gives a paragraph a sense of insistence. The questions can express frustration or concern. They can also plant doubt, hope, or curiosity. And they can highlight the many sides of an issue.

Keep in mind, though, that questions unanswered generally

leave your reader anxious—just as an unresolved chord would. So, one good use of this pattern is in the opening of a piece, to set up questions that you will discuss and answer later.

> But if there is indeed a connection between population and conflict, how does it work? What is its "operational chemistry"? Do population problems directly and inevitably lead to violence? Or do they work indirectly, for example, in catalytic conjunction with other factors such as environmental decline? If the latter, does the "other-factor" complication make population itself less potent as a source of conflict? Or does it make it all the more dangerous, in that population pressures then work in less overt, and hence less heeded, fashion?

Other times, the questions may be merely questioning, rhetorically:

> Should the UN still be trying to put the world to rights? Should it concentrate on social justice? Should it intervene in the civil conflicts that have become more common than wars between states? Should it curl up and die? And, if it is to lead an active life, how can it, when the poor thing is both despised and broke, its major debtors either refusing (the U.S.), or unable (Russia), to pay their bills?

And still other times, the series can support (quite explicitly) the opening point:

> How did things break down? What public ethics reign in a land whose police can kill 111 inmates in a raid on a security prison—and none of the policemen goes to jail, while ten are promoted? Where the head of the tax department has to resign for daring to levy duty on the 17 tons of booty brought back by Brazil footballers last summer with the newly won World Cup?

Where a state governor can walk into a restaurant, shoot his rival, walk away to applause, and win a Senate seat by a landslide? Where society gasps when the president watches carnival arm-in-arm with a semiclad samba dancer, but barely cares that the box he sat in belongs to racketeers?

As these paragraphs show, implication doesn't necessarily mean subtlety. Used occasionally, the pattern can be powerful.

IMPLY THE POINT BY PRESENTING TWO SIDES

Sometimes you may want to present two sides without taking a stand—either because of ignorance or diplomacy. You might also do this to suggest the complexity of a debate, thus allowing you

- to set up your point (choosing one side) in the following paragraph
- to avoid alienating readers when discussing a sensitive issue.

Not many people know it, but India is sitting on a mountain of 30m tonnes of grain; it could increase to 36m tonnes by the end of June, when the wheat harvest ends. *The sceptics say* this merely shows that the poor can no longer afford to buy grain, which is 60% dearer than it was when India started its economic liberalization in 1991. *The supporters of reform retort* that, reform having made many people richer, they are changing their eating habits and switching from cereals to superior foods such as meat, eggs, milk, and vegetables.

Should trade barriers be lowered before, or after, enterprises have been restructured? *Before, say those* who argue that the sudden introduction of freer trade offers domestic monopolies competition from abroad and introduces world prices, helping to correct the price distortions inherited from central planning. *After, say those* who argue that the introduction of foreign competition, though necessary, can be too sudden to allow lumbering domestic enterprises to adjust, threatening a general collapse of output and employment like that seen in East Germany. Poland lowered barriers quickly and now has one of the lowest tariff regimes in the world. Czechoslovakia and Hungary have eliminated most import quotas, though they have retained high tariffs on some products.

In both examples, an issue is presented in the first sentence and then interpreted in two ways. Notice that neither writer signals which side will be taken.

IMPLY THE POINT IN AN ANALOGY OR SYLLOGISM

Analogies and syllogisms can make a topic more engaging. In analogies, A is likened to B: *money* to *water*, *servant* to *financial servant*, and *master* to *industrial master*.

Money is like a body of *water*; a pebble dropped in here, a sluice gate opened there, can send ripples or waves that erode coastlines or flood cities far away. Junk bonds and hostile takeovers are mechanisms and outcomes rather than causes in themselves; building sea walls against them will not deal with their origins. The water will find other ways to transmit the forces which it is carrying.

No man is a hero to his valet: the close and obedient *servant* sees all the weaknesses and vulnerabilities of his *master*. So it is with the *financial servant* and its *industrial master*. Weaknesses in industry and in its political, legal, and social surroundings are observed by the financial system in their finest detail. Worst of all, finance is less discreet than the valet. It passes on its master's frailties for all to see.

More complicated, a syllogism likens A to B, B to C, and thus A to C.

All the *conversational devices* of economics, whether words or numbers, may be viewed as *figures of speech*. They are all metaphors, analogies, ironies, appeals to authority. *Figures of speech* are not mere frills. They *think for us*. Someone who thinks of a market as an "invisible hand" and the organization of work as a "production function" and coefficients as being "significant," as an economist does, is giving the language a great deal of responsibility. It seems a good idea to look hard at this language.

Here the writer has likened *conversational devices of economics* to *figures of speech,* and *figures of speech* (not *mere frills*) to [*things that*] *think for us.*

3

LINK YOUR PARAGRAPHS

Many of the devices that bind sentences within a paragraph — repeating a key term, counting the elements, signaling what's to come, asking and answering questions — can do the same work across paragraphs, creating smooth transitions from one to the next.

REPEAT A WORD OR PHRASE FROM THE END OF THE PRECEDING PARAGRAPH

Words or phrases from one paragraph repeated at the start of the next explicitly tie the two together.

Only 3,100 surnames are now in use in China, say researchers, compared with nearly 12,000 in the past. An "evolutionary dwindling" of surnames is common to all societies, according to Du Ruofu of the Chinese Academy of Sciences; but in China, he says, where surnames have been in use far longer than in most other places, *the paucity has become acute.*

To get an idea of just how *acute,* imagine that the combined populations of the United States and Japan had to make do with but five surnames. That, essentially, is how things are in China, where the five most common surnames—Li, Wang, Zhang, Liu, and Chen—are shared by no fewer than 350 million people. Those named Li alone number 87 million, nearly 8% of the country's Han people, the ethnic Chinese. Another 19 surnames each cover 1% or more of the population.

So far, RNA editing has been seen in marsupials, protozoa, slime moulds, ferns, and flowering plants. Flies *do it*. Mice *do it*. And, it now appears, people *do it*.

Or rather, in most cases, their mitochondria do it. Mitochondria—the cellular machines where glucose is burned for energy—are found in all cells more sophisticated than bacteria. Indeed, many biologists suspect that the ancestors of mitochondria actually were bacteria which gave up an independent life to live symbiotically in early complex cells. They have their own genes, in any case. And these genes are turning out to be heavily edited.

TURN THE REPEATED WORD INTO A QUESTION

Turning the repeated word or phrase at the start of the second paragraph into a question raises an eyebrow of doubt or irony.

Many of the EFF's critics predicted this from the start. The move to Washington in the first place was fiercely controversial among its on-line constituency, whose members worried that the organization would lose touch with its *cultural roots*.

Cultural roots? It may be hard to imagine something as amorphous and all-included as cyberspace having either roots or a culture. But it does. The chief principle of this culture—decentralization—comes from the structure of the Internet, at present cyberspace's main incarnation. The Internet has no real governing body, no real shape, and almost no rules. It is nothing more than a common language by which computers can talk to each other.

In a country with no more arable land than Holland, Egypt has close on 60m people, half of them under 21. True, Egypt's economic indicators are bright—"a *vibrant* economy" is the current official phrase—but economists reckon that it would take a sustained growth rate of 7% or more to soak up the new job-seekers.

Vibrant? With the help of American development aid, parts of the country's infrastructure have been transformed: the telephones miraculously work, there is an electricity surplus, and a new metro system may, eventually, ease serious permanent traffic jams. But investors in Egypt have still to plough through a hideous quagmire of laws, regulations and bureaucracy.

Note how the second paragraphs, without the questions, would have a flat start. The questions thus link the paragraphs and enliven the prose.

REPEAT AN OPENING WORD OR PHRASE

Repeating an opening word or phrase at the beginning of paragraphs propels your argument across two or more of them.

Banks' *credit-risk models* are mind-bogglingly complex. But the question they try to answer is actually quite simple: how much of a bank's lending might plausibly turn bad? Armed with the answer, banks can set aside enough capital to make sure they stay solvent should the worst happen.

No model, of course can take account of every possibility.

Credit-risk models try to put a value on how much a bank should realistically expect to lose in the 99.9% or so of the time that passes for normality. This requires estimating three different things: the likelihood that any given borrower will default; the amount that might be recoverable if that happened; and the likelihood that the borrower will default at the same time others are doing so.

The repeated opening also tells readers that the paragraphs are doing similar work—that the second paragraph adds to or elaborates on the point of the first.

Small wonder, then, that such a variety of insects and plants were unwittingly trapped in the stickiness and thereby preserved, fragmentary DNA and all. The exhibition's 200-odd fossil marvels include entombed ants, a frog, a scorpion, a perfect flower and a yet-to-be-revealed mystery item that Dr Grimaldi discovered recently in New Jersey.

Small wonder, too, that amber has long had cultural significance. Though not especially rare (many trees exuded great gouts of the stuff) it is both attractive and easy to work. Amber has been carved since the Stone Age into symbolic figures and used as currency. The Greeks and Romans alike were fascinated by its weightless luminosity. In recent years the Baltic amber that was expensively transported across Europe to the Mediterranean 2,000 years ago has become ubiquitous as a cheap jewel, exported now as earrings and brooches by modern Balts as desperate as their forebears for trade.

SIGNAL WHAT'S TO COME

Conjunctions and transitional phrases join paragraphs by signaling reversals, continuations, and restatements.

Some of this hand-wringing is disingenuous. Many trade group lobbyists are privately crowing over having outflanked the Administration and the Democratic leadership; the National Federation of Independent Business Inc. (NFIB) send journalists reprints of a *U.S. News & World Report* article touting the small-business lobby's routing of reform legislation.

Nor should the lobbyist's somber demeanor be confused with regret. Most health care industry groups supported only narrow reform proposals of their own design and they clearly preferred inaction to any plan that threatened their members' livelihoods.

But the aftermath of the health care reform battle is unfolding like a bad mystery novel. The victim had dozens of enemies, but now that he's dead, all of them are finding something nice to say about him—and working hard on their alibis. Opinion polls show the public still clamoring for some type of reform, and no group wants to be the target of wrath for this year's inaction.

And gloating isn't a good way to win friends and influence people on Capitol Hill. House Energy and Commerce Committee chairman John D. Dinglee, D-Mich., has promised to hold extensive hearings into the operations of the insurance industry next year—giving a hint of the strained relationships left in the wake of this year's battle.

The best laid plans for the European Union's single currency may yet go astray, but at least the blueprint is on the table. On May 31 the European Commission released its ideas for economic and monetary union (EMU), and proposed a publicity blitz to gain popular support for a three-phase program: the decision to launch the single currency and identify the countries qualified to use it; the "irrevocable" fixing, within a deadline of the following 12 months, of the parities of those countries' currencies; and, within a deadline of three years after that, the transition to the single currency, with its coins and notes introduced "over a few weeks at the most".

In other words, read the Maastricht treaty, which gives starting dates for EMU of 1997 at the earliest and January 1st 1999 at the latest, add a year and then another three, and by 2003 Europeans will be emptying their pockets of marks and francs and filling them with a new Euro-currency.

Though many writers avoid opening a paragraph with a conjunction, as the writer of the second example does, these words are ideal transitional words—they are clear and direct, and tell readers what to expect next.

ESTABLISH PAIRS ACROSS PARAGRAPHS

Similar to repeating a word or phrase, mirroring elements from one paragraph to the next not only aids transition, but links the point of one paragraph to the next.

CIA officials used to have all sorts of irritating habits. If offered a perfectly good *Chateauneuf-du-Pape* at a Georgetown dinner party, they would praise it—by stressing their dissent from the "universal opinion" that unblended reds are better. If told of an especially good *trattoria* in Rome, they might express much gratitude for the information—and deplore their own laziness in always going to the same old Sabatini they had first encountered while vacationing in Italy with their parents. Even more irritating was the propensity of first-generation CIA officials for interjecting into any remotely relevant conversation memories of Groton, Yale, or skiing holidays in St. Moritz.

There is none of that sort of thing anymore. Today's CIA people are not wine snobs—in fact, many of them prefer beer, while others refrain from even coffee, as befits good Mormons. Nor are they partial to foreign foods in funky *trattorias*—

cheeseburgers are more their style. Instead of being Ivy League showoffs, they are quietly proud of their state colleges, however obscure these might be.

What people drink, where they eat, and where they went to school make the point about how CIA officials have changed.

ASK A QUESTION AT THE END OF ONE PARAGRAPH AND ANSWER IT AT THE BEGINNING OF THE NEXT

Questions suggest answers. Posing a question at the end of a paragraph signals the reader to look for your answer in the next.

Having to announce a big drop in profits is not the way any chairman would choose to mark his second week on the job. That was the unenviable task of the new chief of J.P. Morgan, one of America's oldest and mightiest banks, on January 12. Douglas Warner disclosed that the bank's net profit in 1994 was $1.2 billion, 29% less than in 1993. *So why does he look so cheerful?*

Perhaps because he thinks the bank's hardest work has been done. Morgan is at the tail end of a metamorphosis that started in the late 1970s, when this starched commercial bank saw big corporate borrowers turning in their masses from bank loans toward cheaper sources of capital, such as bonds. Under the chairmanship of Sir Dennis Weatherstone, Morgan changed further, concentrating resources on the fee-earning businesses, such as advising clients, and on trading securities. By the end of 1993, noninterest income accounted for 72% of Morgan's earnings, compared with 39% a decade earlier.

A bare two years before the ceremonial opening of St Peter's Holy Door hails the new millennium, Romans are scratching their heads. How can the eternal city cope with an expected influx of millions? Will the traffic flow? Can Rome, even with help from central coffers, afford the sort of projects that the jubilee's organizers deem essential? *Will they, budgets willing, be ready on time?*

Do not bet on it. The space problem is the oldest and worst. For hundreds of years, fragile old Rome has been hard put to embrace a few hundred thousand pilgrims—let alone the 20m–40m expected in the millennial year. Rome lacks vast open spaces. The Piazza San Giovanni, the city's biggest, is chock-full with about 170,000 people; Piazza del Popolo can hold a mere 62,000.

In the second example, a flood of questions gets a simple answer at the start of the second paragraph, quickly dismissing any possibility that Rome might cope.

ASK A QUESTION AT THE BEGINNING OF THE SECOND PARAGRAPH

Opening with a question about the previous paragraph announces that an explanation will follow.

Platinum may be more expensive, troy ounce for troy ounce, but gold remains the noblest metal in the eyes of chemists. Other so-called noble metals react fairly easily with their environment—a copper roof turns green and silver tarnishes—but gold's ability to resist all but the strongest acids is part of the reason it has fascinated kings and commoners for centuries. Even platinum helps other chemicals to react, which is why it is used as a catalyst for car exhausts. Gold, however, remains haughtily above such common tasks, refusing to react with the molecular masses.

But why? It is not as though gold were chemically inert.

After all, anything less than 24-carat gold is an example of gold's ability to bond strongly with other noble metals. The unresolved puzzle has been why oxygen, hydrogen, and other reactive constituents of the atmosphere—and the constituents of many acids—are hard put to bond with gold. Theorists in Denmark now believe that they have the answer. And their calculations do not only provide an explanation for gold's unique pedigree. They also point the way to designing better catalysts.

In other cases, families can afford to send their children to school only if they also work at the same time. It is this family dilemma that makes laws against child labor so difficult to enforce. Thus in Mexico children obtain forged birth certificates in order to secure jobs in the maquiladora factories operated by U.S. firms along the northern border. And it is this that makes worthy corporate codes of conduct liable to backfire: the danger is that, far from contributing to the end of child labor, they merely shift it to shadier areas of the economy that are far harder to police.

So what should companies do? Some initiatives appear more promising than others. One such is the effort that Levi Strauss, a maker of jeans, has made to provide schooling for child workers in its suppliers' plants in Bangladesh. The provision of other benefits, such as medical care and meals, may also be appropriate.

The *Börsen-Zeitung* is among the most expensive daily papers in the world. For the hefty DM 7.20 ($3.80) cover price, readers get the best and most detailed reporting of German companies. The editor, Hans Konradin Herdt, has the sharpest pen of any financial journalist in the country: bound copies of his leading articles are sent to all subscribers as a Christmas present. His satirical talents reduce sober-sided German financiers to stitches. "A silver bullet into the boardroom," is one advertiser's assessment of the paper's reach.

Just who reads it? That, it turns out, is a closely guarded secret. Usually for a newspaper supported by advertising, the *Börsen-Zeitung* refuses to disclose figures, lest they be "misunderstood," Mr. Herdt says. It also declines to commission standard research about its jobs and spending power. Insiders suspect that circulation is small, between 6,000 and 10,000. Simon McPhillips of DMB&B, an advertising agency, says the "ludicrous" lack of information certainly deters advertisers, especially foreign ones.

MAKE A COMMENT

Opening comments—like opening questions—strengthen the link with the preceding paragraph.

Austria, Finland, and Sweden have joined the club. The new members will do no more than tilt the map of Europe a bit to the north and east, but that is proving enough to make those on the southern fringes feel uneasy. They are worried that their concerns will seem relatively unimportant to the northern majority. In particular they fret about North Africa.

With good reason. The Christmas hijacking of an Air France jet by Islamic extremists served as a grim reminder to the French that their former colony, Algeria, is fighting a civil war that may well spill over into France and prompt an exodus of refugees across the Mediterranean. Like France, Spain and Italy already receive a steady flow of illegal immigrants from North Africa, where poverty and fecundity combine to make the adventurous seek a better life in Europe.

Sanctions have recently come to seem the tool of choice in foreign policy. During the cold war, the big task of containing communism was done mainly with tanks and nukes: from 1945 until the break-up of the Soviet Union in 1991, America imposed sanctions less than once a year on average. Now, deprived of a single overarching threat, Americans worry about a range of lesser ones. Few warrant the use of force; all exercise some Washington constituency enough to generate pressure for action. And so, on Mr. Eizenstat's count, America resorted to sanctions 61 times between 1993 and 1996—a frequency 15 times greater than during the cold war.

Up to a point, this is fine. In the past, western sanctions risked driving private countries into the arms of the Soviet Bloc; these days, Russia can be persuaded to go along with sanctions on pariahs like Iraq, so they are more effective. But the rise of sanctions also reflects troubling trends.

The comments—*With good reason* and *Up to a point, this is fine*—could have been made at the end of the first paragraph, but that would have broken the link with the second.

COUNT

Counting is a simple but effective transitional device to link several paragraphs.

However, there are several reasons why the government should be cautious before dipping its hands into taxpayers' pockets. *First,* although charities seem to add significant value at current levels of funding, there is no guarantee that any extra money will produce similar amounts of added value. It may be that charities' income and outputs are around their optimal

level, and that the value added would fall as their income, and therefore their costs, rose.

Second, the study does not look at whether the government agencies or private firms could perform good works more efficiently than charities do. In research comparing care homes for the elderly, Laing & Buisson, a health-care consultancy, has found that charity-run homes are less cost-effective than ones run by for-profit firms. Were this true of good deeds in general, it might be better for the government to hire private contractors to care for vulnerable people, instead of subsiding charities to do so.

First and above all, the "Decline and Fall" is a good history. In its massive erudition, its phenomenal accuracy and its sober judgment it still stands as the indispensable starting point of any study of the Roman empire. *Second,* the work should be read for the majesty of Gibbon's prose. This is eloquence in the grandest manners, cunningly matched to its twin functions of narration and explanation. It is not to be imitated, but to be studied and enjoyed.

PLACE PARAGRAPHS IN TIME

When your paragraphs show a progression in time, use that natural chronology to link them.

In 1969, when relations between China and the Soviet Union were at their worst, China provoked a series of skirmishes, mostly along the Heilongjiang border. Harbin's government, believing a Soviet invasion to be imminent, set about building underground corridors, about three kilometres long, that were meant to house the whole of the city's population in the event of an attack. These were kept meticulously ready until 1985, when peace broke out.

Now they have a new use. The corridors have been turned into a thriving temple of free enterprise selling the latest fashions from Hong Kong. With the shelter the corridors offer from Harbin's −25°C cold, and with the hundreds of jobs this subterranean market has created, they must surely be Russia's greatest gift to the chilly city.

The old model was simple. Information was stored in the DNA of genes. When needed, it was transcribed into template molecules known as messenger RNAs. Then a piece of machinery called a ribosome translated the template, constructing a protein as it went.

Later the model got a bit more complicated. Genes, it was discovered, consist of lengths of informative DNA interspersed with apparently meaningless stretches known as introns. Before a messenger RNA template can be copied into proteins the introns must be removed from it—a process known as splicing.

Now things are getting more complicated still. In the past few years a new phenomenon has been discovered. Sometimes, after the template has been made and the introns removed, the RNA is edited. Sometimes, indeed, it is edited heavily. In the most extreme examples known so far, more than half of the information needed to make a protein has not come from the original gene. Instead, it has been edited into the messenger RNA template.

ANNOUNCE AN EXAMPLE

Some paragraphs illustrate a previous point, opening with *Take* or *Consider* or having a *for example* near the front.

Attacking corporate fat cats has plenty of voter appeal, particularly when few people have yet to feel much benefit from

Britain's economic recovery. But there is no reason to suppose that the bulk of Labour politicians are only pretending to hold these views. And, on their merits, none of these attacks on profitable firms is sustainable.

The IPPR study, *for instance*, criticises the external costs and regional concentrations of supermarket chains using criteria so unreasonable that they would condemn most large industries. The Office of Fair Trading and the Monopolies and Mergers Commission studied supermarkets several times but found no proof of serious market failure or lack of competition.

Once upon a time New York's bankers drank lunch-time martinis; blue-collar Texans drank beer as they cruised the highway; and sophisticates everywhere could tell the difference between bourbon and rye. So much for lost hedonism. Alcohol consumption in America has been declining for the past 17 years, and today no figure with a claim to respectability — politician, businessman or banker — can risk even a single drink at lunch-time. Alcohol is a poison or a distraction; and its use is to be shunned, or indeed restricted.

Last week, *for example*, President Clinton stood beside Brenda Frazier, whose daughter Ashley had been killed by a drunk driver, and announced plans, to apply first on federal property and then across the whole country, to lower the alcohol level at which a driver can still legally drive. "There is hardly a family or community in America", said the president, "that hasn't been touched by drunk driving."

STRING EXAMPLES TOGETHER

You can also string examples together across paragraphs — either to extend them or to contrast them.

Sometimes it irks allies such as the French to see America grab so much of the credit for its mediating efforts. But as even the French admit, America is in a league of its own in this business. No other country can match its clout and its credibility with parties on all sides of an argument. Bosnia is the most striking example: a catastrophe so long as America kept its distance, on the mend once America started to lead.

There are other, less conspicuous examples. Last January an almost comic fracas over a tiny rock in the Aegean briefly threatened to escalate into an alarming conflict between two NATO members, Greece and Turkey. While the European powers looked the other way, and the United Nations called for restraint, the Greeks and the Turks turned to America to help sort the matter out—which, after multiple telephone calls to agitated leaders in Athens and Ankara, it duly did. The next day one of the America diplomats involved, Richard Holbrooke, the star of the Dayton peace talks on Bosnia, described the incident as a microcosm of modern American foreign policy.

But cuts here are political dynamite. Take the government's planned cuts in state help to unemployed and poor people with mortgages, on which spending has grown from £31 in 1979 to £1.1 billion today. Tony Blair, Labour's leader, is determined to stop the cuts. So is Nicholas Winterton, a Tory right-winger keen on cuts in general, who threatens to lead a rebellion against Mr Lilley's plans.

Or take the recent cuts in non-means-tested invalidity benefits. Many of those claiming the benefits are middle-income people who had to retire early and were advised by their employers to top up their pensions with the benefit. And what

are many doing with their new-found leisure? Spending it at Tory coffee mornings, that's what. Mr Lilley has warned colleagues that opposition to cuts in invalidity payments has yet to peak.

UNDERMINE

By undermining the point of the first paragraph, you can propel your argument in the next. You can either be subtle:

> For the first time since 1985, the Geneva-based World Economic Forum has rated the U.S. economy the most competitive in the world. The U.S. Council on Competitiveness, a private coalition of leaders from industry, labor and education, recently concluded that "the United States has significantly strengthened its competitive position in critical technologies during the past five years."
>
> But just like word of Mark Twain's death, *reports of America's industrial revival are exaggerated.* The Sonys, Respironics, and Medrads are isolated islands of success in a sea of economic stagnation. They are what Richard Florida, director of the Center for Economic Development at Carnegie-Mellon University in Pittsburgh, calls deceptive examples of "reindustrialization amidst deindustrialization, pockets of growth that co-exist with the continued decline of some sectors and firms."

or blatant:

> Nippon Steel's Yawata works on the island of Kyushu might stand as a symbol of post-war Japan. In its heyday in the early

1970s, when the economy was still booming and costs were low, the Yawata works employed 46,000. Just 6,400 people work there today. The country's big blast-furnace steel makers have been elbowed aside by minimills, which are technologically more advanced, and by rivals from countries where costs are lower.

There is one catch with this tale: *it is not true.* Although employment has indeed fallen in Japan's five integrated steel makers, they are thriving. Against all expectations, Nippon Steel, Kawasaki Steel, Sumitomo Metal Industries, Kobe Steel and Nippon Kashuha have brought production costs to within a whisker of the world's most efficient producer, South Korea's Pohang Iron & Steel Company (POSCO). The five can now churn out hot-rolled coil at about $300 a tonne compared with POSCO's $270 a tonne.

In the example below, a question does the undermining:

The results are visible on the streets of Warsaw, Prague, and Budapest. Shops are full of western goods. Where grim-faced policemen once stared down pedestrians, street vendors now hawk their wares. The Communist Party's former headquarters in Warsaw houses Poland's infant stock exchange. Prague's Wenceslas Square is festooned with colourful advertisements. Hundreds of thousands of local entrepreneurs have started small businesses. Scores of western law firms, consultants and accountants are setting up offices. From all appearances, business is booming.

Or is it? By most measures, Eastern Europe is in the grip of a prolonged and savage recession. After declining by 8% or so last year, the five countries' GDPs are expected to drop another 8% this year. Industrial output has declined even faster, by 17% last year and probably 11% this year. Like all statistics about Eastern Europe, these figures are endlessly disputed and have to be taken with a large pinch of salt. They may paint too grim a picture because they underestimate the growth of private businesses. Yet these countries are clearly in economic trauma.

EXEMPLARY PARAGRAPHS

Xan Smiley

A G O L D E N A G E O F D I S C O V E R Y

Artificial satellites can read car number
plates. They can photograph pebbles on
mountain-tops. They can gaze into hitherto
unfathomed trenches bigger than the Grand
Canyon in the bowels of the oceans. Loggers,
mineral seekers and road-builders are rolling
back tropical rain forest like a floor rug and
destroying the lives of the world's last "noble
savages." *Ice, mountain, sea, and desert no
longer resist the wiles of modern man and his
machines.*

*The world has shrivelled in the past two cen-
turies.* **It was only in 1806 that** two American
explorers, the unsuitably named Meriwether
Lewis and his friend William Clark, became
the first people (you can bet that no pre-
Columbian personage would have been so
mad) to trudge across the North American
continent. A hundred years ago vast swathes
of Africa were still unknown to outsiders. *It
was only in 1909 and 1912 that* Homo sup-
posedly sapiens managed to stand on the

[margin notes:]
Series of descriptive details

Conclude with the point

Lead with the point

Parallel structure

North and South Poles. Even into the second half of this century, chunks of the world, even people, were unknown to inquisitive industrial man. After the second world war, unheard of peoples—one of them 60,000 strong—living in the highlands and valleys of Papua New Guinea were "contacted" by outsiders for the first time. **Much terra was incognita.**

In the past few decades, the world's remotest places and peoples have been visited, classified, chartered, often desecrated. While vulnerable tribes have died out, backpackers can hitch a ride (not that easily, it is true) across the Sahara. Mount Everest, the world's highest peak, first scaled in 1953, has now been climbed at least 750 times—by 33 people, two years ago, on one day. Tourists have been flown to the North Pole. Eccentrics cross the Atlantic in—as a seriously record-breaking explorer, Sir Ranulph Fiennes, puts it—"ever tinier amphibious bottles of gin."

But hundreds, if not thousands, of peaks and mountain routes are *still* to be climbed. Numerous Arctic and Antarctic challenges are *still* to be met. The rain forests of the Amazon, parts of Africa, New Guinea (that huge island north of Australia made up of Irian Jaya, part of Indonesia, to the west, and Papua New Guinea to the east) all *still* bulge with mystery; *whole ranges of flora, fauna, and even groups of people are scantily known about within them.*

More than 70% of the earth's surface is water; and the oceans, on some measures, are the richest of all places in biodiversity—but

Margin notes:
Conclude with a comment

Lead with the point

Transition: place paragraphs in time

Transition: undermine preceding paragraph

Repeat a word: *still*

Conclude with the point

Imply the point

Point: much about the world is yet unknown

Conclude with a comment

the least known. Only once has a person (or two people together, to be precise) plumbed the depths of the deepest ocean trench. On land and sea, 97% of the world's species have yet—by some recent calculations—to be "discovered." **Yes, 97%.**

Binding: announce and number

*Exploration means many things. **One** is* finding places that have never felt the imprint of a human foot. ***Another*** is satisfying the yen of industrial man to seek out "new" isolated peoples, whose languages or way of life have barely been recorded or analyzed—

Lead with the point; join details using conjunctions

let alone understood. A ***third*** thing usually thought of as belonging with exploration is the feat of human skill or will power among nature's elements, gauged not just by "first visits" to mountain tops or ocean bottoms, but by novel or ever tougher methods of getting there.

Transition: continuation of announce and number

A ***fourth*** type of exploration is scientific. Earth science rather than anthropology or the personal challenges to a man's (and, increasingly a woman's) mind and body against the elements is nowadays perhaps the biggest exploratory motor. To explore—defined in the Oxford dictionary as "to examine (a country, etc.) by going through it" has become more of a "micro" business. These days, mere "going through" is not good enough. Exploration, to more and more people, means examination of whole ecosystems. *In*

Conclude with the point

this respect, most of the world is still up for exploratory grabs.

Lead with the point

The vain, the curious, and the greedy
The old yardsticks still provide the vain, the

philanthropic, the greedy, the religious, the curious, the intrepid and the simply crazy with thousands of challenges not yet met. **Forget,** for a moment, that perhaps 40m species of flora and fauna have yet to be classified. **Think** of the places and even peoples that have never been "discovered," the human feats of travel waiting to be achieved.

Parallel structure: direct address

Most of the world's extremities and most extremely remote places have been visited—but by no means all. **Deserts have been** pretty thoroughly tramped across—though it is surprising how many "firsts," even by car, are not yet in record books. Most of the world's **forests have been,** roughly speaking, visited and mapped. But many have not been scrutinized. At the simplest level, numerous **jungle patches have probably never been** trodden by industrial man before. In Africa, places such as the Ndoki forest, on the border of Congo and Cameroon, or the dense strip of jungle between the Laulaba river (as the upper reaches of the Zaire river, once the Congo, are known) and one of the tributaries, the Lomami, are still virtually unexplored by outsiders. And challenges of survival and travel, especially if you eschew machinery, exist even in well-trodden Africa. It was only in 1986, for instance, that someone (a duo, actually—a similar solo trip has yet to be done) went from west to east by camel across the continent, bisecting the Sahara.

The forests of Borneo, Sarawak and New Guinea, though well traversed in the past two decades, contain pockets of sketchily charted

Lead with the point (point elaborating on point of previous paragraph—building momentum); list disparate details

Parallel structure: one verb form

Conclude
with the
point

territory. *Indeed, all the great jungles of Asia, Africa, and South America, though photographed from the sky, are full of unsolved mystery.*

Point implied in a series of details

The satellite camera cannot peer under the rain forest's canopy, which guards the richest repositories of unknown plant and animal life on land. Only recently have scientists begun to use special cranes and inflatable rafts to snoop into and under the tapestry of the forest roof. Yet the Amazonian ecology is so diverse that some patches, even of an isolated acre or two, may contain species of plants, for instance, that grow nowhere else on the planet. And even when they glimpse the jungle from the sky, the satellites—and their human interpreters—are fallible. Some seemingly authoritative recent atlases, according to John Hemming, director of the Royal Geographical Society, still make "gross errors" in delineating rivers in Amazonia.

Lead with the point; list disparate details

Much is not yet known about the earth's cold bits. As it is landless (though not iceless) for hundreds of miles around the North Pole, the Arctic is also more of a place for the old-fashioned beat-the-elements explorer. Only in 1968 did Wally Herbert, an Englishman, manage the first surface crossing of the Arctic Ocean, from land to land, by way of the North Pole. Nobody, alone, has ever traversed the whole Arctic Ocean, nor gone from one side of the Antarctic continent to the other single-handed, "unsupported" and without mechanical vehicles. Even the rim of Greenland, that large Danish-owned is-

land, has never been circum-navigated—and when a British mountaineer, Chris Bonington, and a fellow explorer, Sir Robin Knox-Johnson, climbed what they thought was the tallest mountain in Greenland in 1991, it turned out that the map-makers had marked the wrong summit. Other exploratory inadequacies are equally revealing: the world's northernmost island, off Greenland was not discovered until 1978.

The Antarctic is sometimes called the "last major unexplored region of the world." Half as big again as the United States, it is valued both for the challenge it still offers to the intrepid and for its trove of undisclosed knowledge sought by the scientist. After the tragi-heroic competition of 1911–12, when a Norwegian, Roald Amundsen, and his team with dogs beat Robert Scott and his five-man team from Britain (all of whom perished) to become the first men at the South Pole, numerous challenges remained to be met. Not until 1993 did a Norwegian, Erling Kagge, become the first person to reach the South Pole, solo, by land and "unsupported."

And whole ranges of Antarctic mountains have never been climbed. Mr. Bonington is heading for one of them soon. One freestanding pinnacle, about 1,000 metres (3,300 feet high) is probably the tallest such tower in the world—unclimbed, of course. **"Very, very exciting,"** he says.

*But scientists are equally **excited** by Antarctica's potential for clues to understanding, among other things, the world's climate.* **To *that* end,** scientists at the European

Project for Ice Coring in Antarctica (EPICA) are embarking on a five-year scheme based at a research station 1,000km (625 miles) from its nearest neighbor, where the average temperature is −45°C. The ice-crust they will investigate is about 3km thick.

A most dangerous sport

Lead with the point; list disparate details

Though seemingly less remote, because more relentlessly explored over many more years, mountains are a source of extraordinary attraction for explorers. Here, too there is a good generation or so to go before anybody can say "everything has been done." Mountaineering is a bizarre activity because it combines so many contradictory feature of humanity: individualism and teamwork, a thirst for survival inspired by a thirst for danger, speed and muscle matched by canniness and steadiness, the practical rubbing against the poetic.

Lead with the point

Two ways to tackle a mountain have been called "the anarchists" and "the organizers." Mountaineers, it hardly needs saying, plan in detail and with ever fancier tackle, how to thwart the elements. Yet many of the hardier ones, rightly in their terms, complain the modern practice is making such heights as Everest too easy. "Doing more with less," is the phrase that mountaineers such as Mr. Bonington like to use. "Easy" here means "not quite so terrifyingly hard." No sport continues to lead so many of the top practitioners to their deaths. "Simple" Everest has killed at least 120 people in the past four decades.

Point implied in a series of details

Not until 1978 did Reinhold Messner, an Austrian who many think is the world's finest living mountaineer, climb Everest in a colleague's company without bottled oxygen. All in all, the most difficult mountain to climb is the world's second tallest, K2, at the western end of the Himalayan range. In 1986, 13 people were killed trying to get up (or down) it. Alison Hargreaves, a Briton who was the first woman up Everest on "normal" air, died on K2 last summer.

Lead with the point; list disparate details

***But** any of the 14 Himalayan peaks which rise to more than 8,000 metres still offer fearsome challenges*; once you have gone up the most straightforward way, new "lines," as mountaineers call their routes, are still to be sought out—though not too many are left. Only two climbers—Mr. Messner was the first—have scaled all 14. The other, a Pole, has since been killed. "Any of those mountains," says Stephen Venables, the first Briton up Everest without extra oxygen, "involves difficult climbing—your mind and body are teetering on the edge of control." And some terrifying unclimbed routes beckon: the west face of K2, the east face of Kanchenjunga, the west face of Makalu (probably the stiffest challenge of the lot), several oxygenless ascents and a number of peak-to-peak ridge traverses.

Transition: begin with a conjunction to link to previous paragraph

Point implied in a series of details

Of the 400 or so peaks between 7,000 and 8,000 metres, more than 100 remain unclimbed. With dollar-desirous China opening its mountains to outsiders, vast new ranges are offering fresh challenges: southeast Tibet, for instance, has a range as long as the Alps (and much taller) where outside professionals have hardly trodden. And the Himalaya is by no means the only range to lure the would-be record-breaker. Some of the Tepui mountains, sheer slabs of unscaled sandstone rising out of the wilderness of southern Venezuela, are magnificently inaccessible.

Another sort that now offers one of the biggest array of possible "firsts" is speleology, better known as caving. One of the world's top cavers, Andrew Eavis, a Briton, reckons that even in Britain, two-thirds of the country's caves have never been penetrated—and across the sea in Ireland, the proportion, he thinks, is 90%. Especially where there is limestone, caves lure the daring and the curious. Aerial photography plus greater geological savvy can predict where they are likely to be. China and New Guinea are prime candidates for a burst of cavernous exploration.

In the densest tropical rain forest of the remote Gunung Mulu National Park in Sarawak (part of Malaysia), **Mr. Eavis** and colleagues found what is the largest known cave in he world: 400 metres long and in places 250 metres high **The Hollywood Bowl could fit inside.** Often the cavers' challenge is to dig to enter: sometimes you must swim underwater through riverine entrances. **Mr. Eavis's** world-beating Sarawak Chamber requires a kilometre-long swim and a waterfall ascent—all in helmet-borne torchlight—before you can reach it. **"We are relatively normal people,"** he says of his fellow speleo-fans.

Margin notes:

Lead with the point; list disparate details

Transition: count

Point implied in a series of details

Comment is conversational

Binding: repetition

Conclude with a comment

The vasty deep

As for the relatively unexplored sea, nobody till recently was able to get far down. Man without mechanical artifice can dip only about ten metres before destroying himself. Even with a "self-contained underwater breathing apparatus" (SCUBA), invented in the 1940s, going 50 metres deep pushes an expert's luck. *Yet the seas are deeper than the mountains are high.* The Mariana trench in mid-Pacific is more than 11,000 metres deep. (Everest, by contrast, is 8,848 metres high). Only two men have ever been there, a French man, Jacques Piccard, and an American, Don Walsh, in the Trieste bathyscope in 1960. Nobody but a Japanese team has been so deep again. **Most scientists say they are not missing much. Only 3% of the ocean is under the 6,000 metre mark.**

All the same, the ocean's average depth is 3,700 metres. And recent discoveries, often by means of remotely operated vehicles (ROVs) and autonomous underwater vehicles (AUVs) show that far more life exists in the deep than most people had guessed. In fact, the oceans almost certainly contain the greatest biodiversity on the planet's surface, whether water-covered or not. New types of bacteria and viruses, as well as an array of new plant and fish life, exist in fantastic abundance: newly discovered sea-worms, mussels, even a huge 20-metre-long squid. Amazingly high temperatures, of more than 400°C have been measured thousands of metres down. Hydrothermal vents are blowing away more than 2,000 metres below sea-level. Sink an-

Margin notes:

Undermine in the middle to make the point

Conclude with a comment

Lead with the point; list disparate details

Transition: undermine previous paragraph

other 1,300 metres, and the Pacific Ocean is carpeted with an array of manganese, cobalt and countless other mineral valuables. Little volcanoes like wobbly black factory chimneys, known as "black smokers," are down there belching out metal sulphides and chemicals.

Most scientists think it not hugely useful for people to be squinting in person at minerals or fish: robots' photographs will do. *But for those seeking new minerals, working out how continents were formed (by plate-tectonics) or predicting climatic and atmospheric change, the ability to explore the depths of the ocean opens a staggering new scientific vista.*

On dry land, exploring for new flora, fauna, and even human life remains as exciting as ever—guess as you might that few or no unknown big animals, let alone peoples, are left. *But you would be wrong there, too.* In Vietnam a completely new species of large mammal, the vu kwang ox (which looks a bit like an oryx), has recently been identified, so has a kind of giant muntjak (something like a fallow deer), and recent whispers from Sumatra suggest a new type of primate may have been found. A leading British ethno-biologist thinks a mega-therium, a sort of giant ground sloth which may stand as high as a giraffe, and was thought to have become extinct several millennia ago, may lurk in the vastnesses of the Amazon basin.

Though less likely, discovering "new people" is also possible. "First contact" yarns ped-

Undermine at the end to make a point

Undermine immediately to make a point

Lead with the point; list examples

dled by fame-seekers have to be listened to warily. "New" peoples are often splinters from "old" ones. But in 1995, both in Irian Jaya and in the Brazilian forest, people previously uncontacted by outsiders may have been found. Over a period of two decades both in the Amazon basin (where 370 or so indigenous groups exist) and in New Guinea (where there are more than a thousand), people unknown to the outside world, some of whose languages were sometimes undeciphered even by their neighbors, have come to light. Study of many well-known peoples living in broadly pre-industrial ways has been so patchy that social anthropologists have eons of research to do—besides which, the people they study never stop evolving into "different" people.

Even in Africa linguists occasionally discover languages never before identified. Defining a language is tricky. Many cover a seamless continuum. But of the 6,528 or so living languages listed by the Summer Institute of Linguistics in Britain, hundreds are not fully understood outside the group that speaks them. *Even in* Nigeria (with 420 languages indexed, out of Africa's 1,995) a tiny new one popped up two years ago. *More worrying, for those who would resist global homogeneity, is languages' galloping disappearance: some linguists reckon that more than 95% may vanish within a century, leaving a shrinking core of some 300 living tongues.* **Many need to be caught on tape before they fly into oblivion.**

Repeat a structure

Undermine at the end to make a point

Conclude with a comment

Discovering yourself

Point implied in a series of details

"The possibilities for exploration and discovery are infinite," says Mr. Hemming. "New species are evolving faster than man can extinguish old ones." Explorers, he believes, are entering "a new golden age of discovery." Although he has experienced hardship and danger (a close friend was killed by Amazonian Indians) during decades of exploration, Mr. Hemming stresses the scientific and philanthropic side—and has fought hard to defend the rights, indeed the survival, of indigenous peoples threatened by modern man.

Lead with the point; list disparate details

Science may now predominate in exploration, but romance, poetry, heroism still call. Even boffins and flea taxonomists may sometimes admit that exploration is also about peering into their souls and asking who they are. Mountaineers, in particular, are unabashed about their urge to compete, both against the horrifying hunks of rock they clamber and often die on, and against their fellow men. Mountaineering, says Mr.

Conclude with comments

Bonington, should not be made "safe, tame, and boring. Man should not overimpose himself on the mountain." Mr. Venables talks of the need to "give the mountain a chance."

Continuation of previous point

Sir Wilfred Thesiger, 85, last of the old school of British explorers, admits even to competing against the indigenous people with whom he lived in the deserts. Among the Rashid of southern Arabia, he candidly admits: "I had to meet the challenge of the desert on equal terms with them. I could

Transition: continuing list of quotations from previous paragraph

equal them physically, the real challenge was to live up to them mentally and morally. But they were the only people I couldn't compete with on a moral level—in honesty, generosity, loyalty, courage. They always thought they were superior to everyone else—and they were."

SOURCES

AN APPROACH TO PARAGRAPHS

Getting off to a good start

Still an Unequal World, Human Development Report (Washington, D.C.: United Nations Development Programme, 1995), p. 29.

"Clearing the Killing Fields," *The Economist* 347, no. 8066 (2 May 1998): 73.

"Word of Mouse," *The Economist* 347, no. 8066 (2 May 1998): 57.

W. John Moore, "An Albatross Named Bill," *National Journal* 26, no. 42 (15 October 1994): 2406.

Solange De Santis, "Nice Bagpipes, Man, But Don't You Feel a Draft in That Skirt?" *Wall Street Journal,* 12 October 1994, sec. A, p. 1.

Paul Krugman, "Not for Ordinary Folk," (www.redherring.com/mag/school.html) issue 38.

"Triumphant abroad," in *Survey: Asia's Emerging Economies, The Economist* 321, no. 7733 (16 November 1991): 7.

Meg Greenfield, "Unsexing the Military," *Newsweek* 129, no. 24 (16 June 1997): 80.

E. M. Forster, *Aspects of the Novel* (New York: Harcourt, Brace, 1955), p. 83.

Summing up

A. Leon Higginbotham, Jr., "Breaking Thurgood Marshall's Promise," *New York Times Magazine,* 18 January 1998, sec. 6, p. 29.

Jonathan Broder, "Tangier," *Smithsonian* 29, no. 4 (July 1988): 100.

"The Last Communists," *The Economist* 346, no. 8051 (17 January 1998): 21.

"From Morgan's Nose to Milken's Wig," in *Survey: International Finance, The Economist* 319, no. 7704 (27 April 1991): 12.

"The Somali Spectre," *The Economist* 333, no. 7883 (1 October 1994): 20.

1. UNIFY YOUR PARAGRAPHS AROUND STRONG POINTS

Be clear about your subject

"Where the Old China Lives On," *The Economist* 334, no. 7897 (14 January 1995): 33.

"The Interminable Net," *The Economist* 338, no. 7951 (3 February 1996): 70.

Make a strong point

"Sacking the Powers-That-Be," *The Economist* 333, no. 7884 (8 October 1994): 99.

"No Going Back," *The Economist* 335, no. 7917 (3 June 1995): 17.

"China Odyssey," *The Economist* 337, no. 7937 (21 October 1995): 91.

Be sure every sentence bears on the point

"Nobel Game Theory," *Wall Street Journal*, 12 October 1994, sec. A, p. 14.

Stephen Kinzer, "A Climate for Demagogues," *Atlantic* 273, no. 2 (February 1994): 21–22.

"Risk and Reward," in *Survey: Asia's Emerging Economies, The Economist* 321, no. 7773 (16 November 1991): 6.

Repeat a key term

"The Death of Distance," *The Economist* 336, no. 7934 (30 September 1995): 6–7.

"Scribble, Scribble, Mr Gibbon," *The Economist* 334, no. 7897 (14 January 1995): 75.

David Shribman, "Mr. Speaker," *New York Times Book Review*, 21 April 1996, sec. 7, p. 15.

Repeat a sentence structure—for sentences doing the same work

David Shribman, "Mr. Speaker," *New York Times Book Review*, 21 April 1996, sec. 7, p. 15.

"If Wall Street Falters," *The Economist* 340, no. 7973 (6 July 1996): 19.

Herbert Stein, "High Life on the Potomac," *Slate* (www.slate.com) 17 April 1997.

Count the elements

Herbert Stein, "Reading the Inaugurals," *Slate* (www.slate.com), 10 January 1997.

"Still an Unequal World," The Human Development Report 1995 (New York: Oxford University Press, 1995), p. 29.

"Just Like Ringing a Bell," in *Survey: The Music Business. The Economist* 321, no. 7738 (21 December 1991): 4.

Signal what's to come

"Can Labour Learn to Love Profit?" *The Economist* 334, no. 7897 (14 January 1995): 49.

"The Voice of Economic Nationalism," *Atlantic* 282 no. 1 (July 1998): 100.

"The Shan Connection," *The Economist* 338, no. 7947 (6 January 1996): 27.

Stick to one subject

"Endicott Peabody," *The Economist* 345, no. 8047 (13 December 1997): 80.

"How to Kill Your Multimedia Industry," *The Economist* 333, no. 7889 (12 November 1994): 87.

"It Seems to Me," *Slate* (www.slate.com), 6 February 1997.

Stick to one verb form

"Paradise Retained," *The Economist* 338, no. 7951 (3 February 1996): 72.

Henry R. Luce, *The American Century* (New York: Farrar and Rinehart, 1941), p. 32.

2. MAKE YOUR POINTS IN COMPELLING WAYS

Lead with the point and support it

"Unjammed," *The Economist* 347, no. 8069 (23 May 1998): 74.

Ken Wells, "The Ancient Baobab Is a Sight to Behold, and That's the Rub," *Wall Street Journal*, 20 March 1997, sec. A, p. 1.

"For Richer, for Poorer," *The Economist* 333, no. 7888 (5 November 1994): 20.

Lead with the point and conclude with a comment

"Geo-political Earthquake," *The Economist* 335, no. 7917 (3 June 1995): 45.

Thomas T. Samaras, "Let's Get Small," *Harper's* 289, no. 1736 (January 1995): 32–33.

"Banking on the Fed," *The Economist* 337, no. 7937 (21 October 1995): 80.

"The Fundamentals of Editing," *The Economist* 338, no. 7957 (16 March 1996): 82.

"At Last, a People's Art," *The Economist* 346, no. 8051 (17 January 1998): 77.

Lead with the point and, using conjunctions, join details

"The Trouble with Teams," *The Economist* 334, no. 7897 (14 January 1995): 61.

"Blood Disorder," *The Economist* 338, no. 7958 (23 March 1996): 49.

Lead with the point and list disparate details

Jeffrey Goldberg, "Our Africa," *New York Times Magazine*, 2 March 1997, sec. 6, p. 76.

"One Swallow," *The Economist* 342, no. 8009 (22 March 1997): 65.

Lead with the point and follow it with a bulleted list

UNDP–World Bank, *Water and Sanitation Program Annual Report,* July 1994–June 1995 (Washington, D.C.: World Bank, 1996), pp. 64–65.

UNDP, *Human Development Report 1995* (New York: Oxford University Press, 1995), p. 39.

Conclude with the point after introducing the subject

"Slicing the Cake," *The Economist* 333, no. 7888 (5 November 1994): 13.

Paul Krugman, "The CPI and the Rat Race," *Slate* (www.slate.com), 21 December 1996.

Conclude with the point after listing disparate details

"To Bury or to Praise," *The Economist* 337, no. 7937 (21 October 1995): 23.

"The Mall of Dreams," *The Economist* 339, no. 7964 (4 May 1996): 23.

Make the point in the middle

"The Aspic of History," *The Economist* 338, no. 7947 (6 January 1996): 67.
Richard Rorty, "Demonizing the Academy," *Harper's* 289, no. 1736 (January 1995): 13.

Undermine a premise at the end of a paragraph

"The Age of Social Transformation," *Atlantic* 274, no. 5 (November 1994): 64.
"Owners vs. Managers," *The Economist* 333, no. 7884 (8 October 1994): 20.

Undermine a premise immediately

Russell Jacoby, "The Ivory Tower Obscurity Fetish," *Harper's*, 289, no. 1732 (September 1994): 26.
Herbert Stein, "The Cubist Republican," *Slate* (www.slate.com), 15 May 1997.

Undermine a premise in the middle of the paragraph

"The Age of Social Transformation," *Atlantic* 274, no. 5 (November 1994): 59.
"Under New Management," *The Economist* 333, no. 7884 (8 October 1994): 21.

Start with a question and answer it immediately

"Short Guys Finish Last," *The Economist* 337, no. 7946 (23 December 1995): 19.
"The Survival of the Fittest," *The Economist* 337, no. 7937 (21 October 1995): 92.
"Doubts, Hesitancy, Determination," *The Economist* 346, no. 8055 (14 February 1998): 51.
"A Sobering View," *The Economist* 334, no. 7897 (14 January 1995): 74.

Start with a question and answer it in succeeding sentences

"The Poor Get Richer," *The Economist* 333, no. 7888 (5 November 1994): 39.
Marcy Lamm, "A New York Court May Decide When a Cough Drop Gets Stale," *Wall Street Journal*, 18 June 1996, sec. B, p. 1.

Start with a question and answer it at the end

"The Philosopher's Pupil," *The Economist* 338, no. 7948 (13 January 1996):
77.

"On the Rocks," in *East Asian Economies Survey*, *The Economist* 346, no.
8058 (7 March 1998): 7.

Ask several questions and answer each immediately

"To Bury or to Praise," *The Economist* 337, no. 7937 (21 October 1995): 27.

Paul Krugman, "In Praise of Cheap Labor," *Slate* (www.slate.com), 20
March 1997.

Imply the point in a series of details or examples

"The Ups and Downs of Two Italian Rivals," *The Economist* 342, no. 8008
(15 March 1997): 56.

Andrew Jacobs, "Where Prices Are out of This World," *New York Times*, 18
November 1997, sec. A, p. 16.

Imply the point in a series of questions

Norman Myers, *Ultimate Security: The Environmental Basis of Political
Stability* (Washington D.C.: Island Press, 1993), p. 153.

"To Bury or to Praise," *The Economist* 337, no. 7937 (21 October 1995):
23.

"A Disease of Society," *The Economist* 333, no. 7888 (5 November 1994):
48.

Imply the point by presenting two sides

"How to Sit on a Useless Pile," *The Economist* 335, no. 7917 (3 June 1995):
33.

Bruce Stokes, "Out of the Rubble," *National Journal* 26, no. 42 (15
October 1994): 2398.

Imply the point in an analogy or syllogism

"From Morgan's Nose to Milken's Wig," in *Survey: International Finance*,
The Economist 319, no. 7704 (27 April 1991): 12.

"Your Obedient Servant," in *Survey: International Finance*, *The Economist*
319, no. 7704 (27 April 1991): 43.

Deirdre N. McCloskey, *The Rhetoric of Economics* (Madison: University of
Wisconsin Press, 1985), p. 3.

3. LINK YOUR PARAGRAPHS

Repeat a word or phrase from the end of the preceding paragraph

"O Rare John Smith," *The Economist* 335, no. 7917 (3 June 1995): 32.
"The Fundamentals of Editing," *The Economist* 338, no. 7957 (16 March 1996): 81.

Turn the repeated word into a question

"Who Speaks for Cyberspace?" *The Economist* 334, no. 7897 (14 January 1995): 64.
"Sad Dreams by the Nile," *The Economist* 335, no. 7917 (3 June 1995): 35.

Repeat an opening word or phrase

"Model Behaviour," *The Economist* 346, no. 8057 (28 February 1998): 80.
"The Aspic of History," *The Economist* 338, no. 7947 (6 January 1996): 67.

Signal what's to come

Julie Kosterlitz, "The Second Wave," *National Journal* 26, no. 42 (15 October 1994): 2393.
"Fazed," *The Economist* 335, no. 7917 (3 June 1995): 69.

Establish pairs across paragraphs

Edward Luttwak, "The CIA Is Déclassé," *Slate* (www.slate.com), 29 March 1997.

Ask a question at the end of one paragraph and answer it at the beginning of the next

"A Blue Chip on a New Block," *The Economist* 334, no. 7897 (14 January 1995): 65.
"Italy's Millennial Tangle," *The Economist* 345, no. 8047 (13 December 1997): 46.

Ask a question at the beginning of the second paragraph

"Gold: A Repulsive Metal but a Noble One," *The Economist* 335, no. 7917 (3 June 1995): 76.
"Consciences and Consequences," *The Economist* 335, no. 7917 (3 June 1995): 13.

"Germany's 'Silverbullet,' " *The Economist* 346, no. 8051 (17 January 1998): 69.

Make a comment

"Mediterranean Blues," *The Economist* 334, no. 7897 (14 January 1995): 14.

"The Many-Handed Mr. Eizenstat," *The Economist* 346, no. 8052 (24 January 1998): 30.

Count

"Valuing Virtue," *The Economist* 347, no. 8070 (30 May 1998): 57.

"Scribble, scribble Mr. Gibbon," *The Economist* 334, no. 7897 (14 January 1995): 75.

Place paragraphs in time

"The Russians Are Coming," *The Economist* 334, no. 7897 (14 January 1995): 34.

"The Fundamentals of Editing," *The Economist* 338, no. 7957 (16 March 1996): 81.

Announce an example

"Can Labour Learn to Love Profit?" *The Economist* 334, no. 7897 (14 January 1995): 49.

"Let the Law, at Least, Be Clearheaded," *The Economist* 346, no. 8059 (14 March 1998): 25.

String examples together

"Leadership on the Cheap," *The Economist* 339, no. 7964 (4 May 1996): 30.

"Principles of Surgery," *The Economist* 334, no. 7897 (14 January 1995): 52.

Undermine

Bruce Stokes, "Out of the Rubble," *National Journal* 26, no. 42 (15 October 1994): 2398.

"On a Roll," *The Economist* 345, no. 8038 (11 October 1997): 74.

"Jam Tomorrow," in *Survey: Business in Eastern Europe, The Economist* 320, no. 7725 (21 September 1991): 4.

EXEMPLARY PARAGRAPHS

"A Golden Age of Discovery," *The Economist* 337, no. 7946 (23 December 1995): 56–58.

PART THREE

RIVETING

AN APPROACH TO PLANNING AND DRAFTING   203

1 FIGURE OUT WHAT YOU'RE WRITING AND FOR
   WHOM   208
   What's your main topic?   208
   Who's going to read what you write?   210
   What's your purpose in writing?   211
   How long should your report be?   213
   How much time can you spend writing?   214
   What's your working title?   215

2 SPELL OUT YOUR MAIN AND SUPPORTING
   MESSAGES   218
   Your main message   219
   Your supporting messages   220

3 USE YOUR SUPPORTING MESSAGES TO
   DEVELOP AN OUTLINE   225

4 DECIDE HOW LONG EACH SECTION WILL BE   229

5 CREATE A PARAGRAPH-BY-PARAGRAPH PLAN   232

6 MAKE A STRONG POINT ABOUT EACH OF
YOUR PARAGRAPH TOPICS   234

7 GATHER YOUR DETAILS, EXAMPLES, AND
COMMENTS   237

8 CONVERT YOUR RAW MATERIAL INTO DRAFT
PARAGRAPHS   239
    Lead with the point and support it   240
    Lead with the point and conclude with a
    comment   241
    Lead with the point and follow it with a
    bulleted list   241
    Conclude with the point after introducing the
    subject   242
    Start with a question and answer it immediately   243

9 TAPE YOUR DRAFT ON A WALL TO APPLY THE
FINISHING TOUCHES   244
    Review your line of argument   245
    Spotlight your messages   245
    Adjust length and balance   245
    Refine your title and section headings   246
    Take a last look   247

EXEMPLARY REPORTS: FROM START TO FINISH   248
    Topic, audience, and purpose   248
    Messages   249
    Outline headings   250
    Paragraph plan   250
    Sample paragraph contents   251
    First draft   252

EXEMPLARY REPORTS: FROM PLAN TO DRAFT   256

SOURCES   267

AN APPROACH TO PLANNING
AND DRAFTING

MOST writers start by assembling details, examples, and comments in paragraphs—sporadically making points, rarely conveying a message. The approach here is to do the reverse—to start with your messages, to support them with points, and to use those points to assemble your details, examples, and comments.

What I suggest here is that you begin by answering a few basic questions about your topic, audience, and purpose. Next, come up with your main message and three or four supporting messages. Then use those messages to develop an outline, and move beyond that outline to formulate a detailed paragraph-by-paragraph plan for your first draft.

This may seem overly systematic, but it is just a plan, and plans change. The idea is to give your report a strong, linear foundation—and to save time when it comes to writing.

Coming up with your main and supporting messages before you start writing may seem impossible (the mere thought of it makes some writers catatonic). But what better way to structure your report than to have your messages provide your outline?

The techniques in this part are one set among many for

preparing to write. Not all people can systematically plan what they are going to write before they start drafting, and many have to start writing just to get a feel for what they're dealing with. There's no reason to deny such spontaneity. But if you're in this school, try setting your first outpouring to one side and using it as raw material for the planning and drafting techniques described here.

If you normally produce an outline before you begin writing, first try answering the six questions in Chapter 1 of this part. If you already have an outline, see how you might improve it after you've answered those questions. Then read on to see how you can open your outline into a paragraph-by-paragraph plan.

If you write from a stack of index cards covered with notes, the techniques suggested here can help you to assemble those notes. The plan you develop will help you decide which bits of your raw material fit where and which don't fit at all.

You can also use these techniques at various points in the writing process and in various situations:

- Before you write—obviously the best time to plan
- After you write—to get a sense of the structure, balance, and linearity of your argument
- If you're asking someone to write something—to have them make it perfectly explicit what they will deliver
- If you're being asked to write something—to establish a "contract" for what you will deliver and to avoid a manager's capricious changes of mind
- If you're writing with others—to avoid overlap and to have a clear idea of what your colleagues are covering in their sections or chapters

And now, the nine steps to planning and drafting your riveting report:

Step 1. Figure out what you're writing and for whom. Start by answering six simple questions. What's your main topic? Who's going to read what you write? What's your purpose in writing? How long should your report be? How much time can you spend writing? What's your working title?

Step 2. Spell out your main and supporting messages. The most important sentence in any piece of writing spells out the main message. The problem is, few writers know what their main message is, and, if they do, they either don't write it down or they bury it in the conclusion. Identifying your main message forces you to boil down everything you want to communicate about a topic into one statement. It can be descriptive or prescriptive, and you should be able to voice it easily in 25 or so words. A short piece of writing may have no supporting messages, only a series of points to support the main message. A long piece generally needs supporting messages, to make your argument clear. But avoid more than three or four if you want people to remember them.

Step 3. Use your supporting messages to develop an outline. This way your outline and headings will reinforce—and resonate with—your messages. Your main message should drive your title, and your supporting messages should drive your section headings, which generally are needed in pieces longer than a couple of pages.

Step 4. Decide how long each section will be. Given the overall page length that you've decided at the outset, assign those pages to individual sections. Because the page is merely a unit of display, try to convert those pages to numbers of paragraphs. If you're writing 10 double-spaced pages, that's around 25 paragraphs. If 15, that's around 40.

Step 5. Create a paragraph-by-paragraph plan. To each paragraph, assign the topic that you need to cover, expanding your outline of section (and possibly subsection) headings into a paragraph-by-paragraph plan. Keep in mind that this is just a start—that some paragraph topics will disappear, others will expand to two or three paragraphs.

Step 6. Make a strong point about each of your paragraph topics. To turn those topics into points, write each of them at the top of a page or screen. If you have 30 paragraph topics, you'll need 30 sheets of paper or 30 screens. Now, make a strong point about each topic in 25 to 30 words. Assembled, this clothesline of points is your full line of argument.

Step 7. Gather your details, examples, and comments. On each page, under each point, make notes to assemble your details, examples, and comments. And to make it easier to shoot down your birds of thought on the wing, spread all your pages out on a table or carry them around in a binder.

Step 8. Convert your raw material into draft paragraphs. After you've assigned all your examples, details, and other supportive material to each point, you are finally ready to begin writing. Each page of raw material can now be drafted into sentences to build a coherent paragraph. See Part Two, *Powerful Paragraphs*, for tips on writing paragraphs that are unified, coherent, and well developed.

Step 9. Tape your draft on a wall to apply the finishing touches. The perspective of seeing an entire draft at one glance is more illuminating than you can imagine—far more so than looking at one page at a time. With your draft taped on a wall or spread out on the floor, you can check the balance of your sections, review your line of argument, make sure your messages stand out, review your headings, and get rid of anything that doesn't fit.

So, planning means having more than a rough outline to guide your writing. It also means identifying your messages, organizing your report into sections and subsections, and arranging those sections in the most persuasive and logical order. And it means deciding the point of each paragraph—and gathering the details and examples you will call on to support each point—before you begin writing. *Drafting* thus means writing from a plan. It means making sure that your main and supporting messages are clear to your readers, and that the point of each paragraph is clear and well supported.

1

FIGURE OUT WHAT YOU'RE WRITING AND FOR WHOM

BEFORE you develop your messages and put together an outline, try to answer the following six questions—questions that writers seldom have clear answers to even after they've finished writing: What's your main topic? Who's going to read what you write? What's your purpose in writing? How long should your report be? How much time can you spend writing? What's your working title?

WHAT'S YOUR MAIN TOPIC?

Your first answer will likely be broad, so take the time to be more specific. Clearly specifying your topic narrows the boundaries of what your report will cover and keeps it from rambling or unraveling.

The first answer a team at the Census Bureau gave for a policy brief to be drawn from a massive compilation of data:

Population growth

After a bit of probing, we narrowed it to:

Projected growth of the U.S. population by state between 1995 and 2025

I immediately had a clear picture of what the policy brief would cover.

The first answer a team at the World Bank came up with for a chapter in the *World Development Report* on knowledge for development was just that:

Knowledge for development

Well, there are many kinds of knowledge and lots of development, past and prospective, so we narrowed the topic to:

Nurturing local and global networks of people marshaling knowledge for human and economic development

That later changed, but at least it began to sharpen the focus.

I once had a pair of authors who wanted me to give them a hand in putting together a book summing up three years of work in developing a new survey method. To my deceptively simple question, one of them answered:

A guide for policymakers on how to interpret the survey's findings

To which the other said, "No, no, no." Instead, the topic was:

A manual for statisticians on how to conduct such a survey

They went back and forth on this for about an hour, so I left. They ended up writing two books, each on his own.

Start by writing—then refining—the first words that come into your head. Then ask yourself the usual who? what? when?

where? how? Avoid such phrases as *a report on, a review of, an analysis of,* which can distract you from a clear statement of your topic. And test your topic on a few colleagues to see if they understand it or have something to add.

WHO'S GOING TO READ WHAT YOU WRITE?

One person or a thousand? Your supervisor or your subordinates? A small circle of experts or the public? Identifying your audience often helps you determine what you'll write and how you'll write it. It determines, in part, what sort of language to use — formal or informal, direct or diplomatic, neutral or persuasive. It also determines the length and organization of your report.

You'd be amazed at the number of times writers tell me they don't know who the audience is. Their first crack at answering is usually vague:

Policymakers

And after a bit of discussion they might identify:

Senior treasury officials responsible for international affairs

Each year the team of economists putting together the World Bank's *World Development Report* starts with something like:

Government officials

to which they add:

People in the development community more broadly

And with a bit of reflection, they add:

The press, graduate students, those in nongovernmental organizations, the public

pushing them up to 6 billion people. So we then separate their core audience:

A roundtable of key ministers in developing countries

and their secondary audiences:

Economics editors in the media, specialists in development agencies, professors and graduate students in universities

Begin by listing the people you most want to read your report from start to finish, add the people who you know will read it, then continue by adding the names of those people whose interest you would like to attract. (Don't forget to add the names of your supervisors and other reviewers.) Avoid nondescript labels, and try to identify representatives from each of your audiences. Name names, if you can. Then broaden to titles of organizations, institutions, and populations. If you are writing for more than one audience, try to distinguish your primary audience from your secondary audience.

WHAT'S YOUR PURPOSE IN WRITING?

Some reports have a clear purpose: interpreting the results of a study, introducing a new policy. Others may have lost their purpose, such as annual reports that are done the same way every year. Still others, such as fund-raising requests, mask their purpose intentionally.

For that Census Bureau policy brief I mentioned earlier, the first statement of purpose was:

To inform the public about U.S. census projections

After considerable pushing, we narrowed it:

To persuade state and local governments that the population projections provide a sound basis for planning

It's easy to inform. It's not easy to persuade. And almost all reports are meant to persuade someone of something.

For a policy report by the Benton Foundation and Libraries for the Future, the first attempt at the purpose was:

To show the importance of libraries in the digital age

That was quickly refined to this:

To persuade librarians, policymakers, foundations, and corporations of the importance of libraries as resource centers for the new communications and information tools in this digital age

Compare the timid *show the importance of* with the stronger *persuade*, surrounded by concrete detail.

So, to say that you are writing to *inform* your audience about your topic is not enough: there is almost always another purpose.

The following verbs all avoid the specific:

communicate
emphasize
describe
explore
tell
consider
suggest

while these verbs can push you toward greater detail and clarity:

create
persuade
promote
take
convince
force
motivate
quell
change
push

If you're having trouble identifying your purpose, ask yourself: What do you want your audience to do after reading your report? Adopt your recommendations? Formulate a new set of policies? Change their behavior? Sometimes your purpose may have a hidden agenda—to get a promotion or change the way your department is organized.

HOW LONG SHOULD YOUR REPORT BE?

Or better still: How much time will your audience devote to reading it? If only 10 minutes, your report should be about 10 double-spaced pages. It may be hard to chop 90 pages off your planned 100-pager, but remember that few people read an entire report, no matter how riveting, and that shorter reports are usually tighter—and better written.

Many people come up with an imprecise estimate:

However long it ends up

or:

Around 10 to 20 pages

Much more useful is:

10 double-spaced pages of typescript

On average, your readers cruise along at about 250 words a minute, or roughly 1 double-spaced page a minute. So if your audience is spending 10 minutes on your report, that's 2,500 words, or 10 double-spaced pages.

That's precisely what we came up with for a report on urban poverty for the Rockefeller Foundation. Millions of dollars in research. Thousands of pages of write-ups. Twelve researchers and project managers sitting around a conference table, thinking, no doubt, that their policy report would run 100 to 200 pages. But the discipline of tailoring the length of the report to the attention that it might command from legislators and senior administration officials led us to 10 double-spaced pages.

Once you have an estimate of the number of pages (units of display), try to convert that into numbers of paragraphs (units of composition). If you're writing 10 double-spaced pages, that's roughly 25 paragraphs (at 2.5 per page). And if you're writing 10 single-spaced pages, that's roughly 40 paragraphs (at 4 per page).

If the length of your report gets out of hand, prepare an executive summary. And if the summary gets too long for your core audience, try a cover note that presents your messages.

HOW MUCH TIME CAN YOU SPEND WRITING?

Writing, at least the writing of reports, is usually preceded by the separate processes of research and analysis. Keep that in mind when estimating the amount of time you will spend on a report. Also keep in mind that other things are sure to intrude on your time.

Here, too, people are imprecise:

As long as it takes

Compare that with:

First draft: 5 days, 8 hours a day, to be finished May 1.
Revised final draft: 3 days, 4 hours a day, to be finished May 15.

Give your estimate in clock time rather than calendar days, and think about multiplying that estimate by 2 or 3 to account for optimism and unexpected interruptions.

Because most people squeeze writing in at the end of the research-analysis-writing cycle, try to begin planning before you start writing, during the analysis and even the research, and include time for review and revision.

WHAT'S YOUR WORKING TITLE?

The title is your first chance to engage your reader, so be brief, honest, and communicative.

Compare this first attempt:

African Import Prices: 1970, 1980, and 1990

with this final:

Do African Countries Pay More for Their Exports? Yes

The title made the difference for a World Bank working paper, reviewed by every major African newspaper as well as London's *Financial Times.*

Another conventional title:

Strategies for Implementing Reform

injected with a bit of urgency:

Reform Can't Wait

And a typically bureaucratic title:

Economic Growth and Public Investment

made a bit more engaging:

From Boom to Bust—and Back?

The overview of a recent *Human Development Report* had this as the title of its opening chapter:

Overview

But it was the following title that put the overview on the map:

The Revolution for Gender Equality

Here's another title that may have been true:

A Comparative Analysis of Commodity-Dependent Economies in Developing Countries but that became the subtitle for the more memorable:

Plundering Agriculture

The best titles are memorable and easy to repeat. A *Comparative Analysis of Commodity-Dependent Economies in Developing Countries* did not fall trippingly off the tongue, but *Plundering Agriculture* remains in readers' minds years after publication.

In your titles, avoid words like:

procedures for
overview of
experiment in
review of
findings of
summary of
report on
issues surrounding
strategy for
implications of
investigation into

And don't get stuck with your first working title, as most writers do. Instead, continually scrutinize your working title to see how you can further refine it to be true to your messages and readers.

2

SPELL OUT YOUR MAIN AND SUPPORTING MESSAGES

FEW writers think of the messages they are trying to communicate in a report. That is why I also try to spell out the main message in 25 to 30 words and three or four supporting messages, each of them in 25 to 30 words. The idea is to build a hierarchy: main message → supporting messages → points (one to a paragraph) → details, examples, and comments. Most writers wallow in the details, occasionally making a point, rarely voicing a message.

One reason they wallow is that it's not easy to spell out messages. I once spent six hours with a high-powered team at the Federal Reserve Board trying to come up with the message structure for a five-year strategic plan. The team thought that four sentences in six hours was wildly unproductive, but they had much more: agreement by all of them for the first time on what the plan should cover.

In coming up with your messages, will you move from the general to the specific? Will you divide a problem into its parts or provide solutions to a problem? Will you describe a process? (For more on shaping your argument, see Chapter 3.) And as you temporize with supporting messages, decide how to arrange them. You should also check to be sure that one of your supporting messages isn't really your main message.

YOUR MAIN MESSAGE

The most important question about any piece of writing is: *What is the main message you want to convey?* The main message is the single most important idea that you want your reader to walk away with. Answering this question forces you to boil down into one statement everything you know about your topic and everything you hope to achieve by writing about it. If *you* don't articulate it, your reader certainly won't be able to.

As with the title, the main message will help you decide what to keep and what to cut by defining the boundaries of your report. Also like the title, the main message should do more than describe or inform—it should compel. Don't leave your readers in suspense. Remember, they may not have much time to read your report. Use simple language, and load value into your main message. Also remember that supporting messages follow, so don't overload it.

Messages classify and describe things (descriptive messages) or recommend action (prescriptive messages).

Some first attempts at a main message are too general:

New technology can have a beneficial effect on communities.

so think about adding a bit of detail:

New communications technologies can strengthen neighborhoods, create new opportunities for participation in civic affairs, and promote economic development on a scale that enhances, rather than undermines, life in communities.

Some attempts at coming up with the main message leave the reader with a *So what?*

> Economic policies are often dominated by political considerations.

This can often be fixed by adding a *Because* to the front of the first statement and continuing with the action recommended:

> Because economic policies are often dominated by political considerations, economists must maintain contact with their roots and be more willing to accept innovation and change.

What do you really want to say? Keep the answer short and simple—you should be able to voice it easily. And try reading your main message aloud to colleagues to see if they can repeat it back to you. If they can't, the message may be too long (more than 30 words?), too vague, or too complicated.

YOUR SUPPORTING MESSAGES

A short piece of writing may not have supporting messages, relying instead on a series of points to support the main message. A longer piece generally needs supporting messages, but you should avoid having more than three or four if you want your readers to remember them. Your supporting messages divide your argument and thus become the conceptual architecture that informs your outline.

Here's the main message for that Rockefeller Foundation report I mentioned in Chapter 1:

Higher program participation, higher placement in jobs, higher pay—these are the payoffs possible from an integrated program of education and employment that can be delivered at reasonable cost.

And here are the supporting messages:

Job training should develop specific work skills.

Basic skills training should be related to the job.

Education and employment programs should be tied to the requirements of industry.

Those programs should also be tailored to the individual.

Training should be surrounded with a full array of support services.

These five sentences are the essence of what the research team wanted to communicate to legislators and program administrators. It took 12 people half a day to come up with them.

Here, the main message for the *World Development Report 1997*:

An effective, capable state is vital for the provision of the goods and services, rules, and institutions that allow markets to flourish and people to lead healthier, happier lives.

And here, the supporting messages:

To make the state a more effective partner in a country's development, the state's role should be matched to its capability.

Raising a state's capability so that it reinvigorates public institutions means first designing effective rules and restraints that check arbitrary state actions and combat entrenched corruption.

Removing obstacles to state reform will only succeed if efforts are directed by leaders with a clear vision of the way things could be, and a contagious determination to turn that vision into reality.

In a World Bank report for governments and the media in the Middle East and North Africa, the main message set the challenge echoed in the report's title, *Claiming the Future*:

By 2010 the countries of the Middle East and North Africa have the potential to double incomes, increase life expectancy by close to 10 years, and cut illiteracy and infant mortality by almost half.

And the supporting messages elaborated on the promise:

They could become full partners in the global economy using integration with Europe and within the region as a stepping stone to international competitiveness.

The faster economic growth would reduce poverty and bring down unemployment, restoring hope to millions.

Peace, macroeconomic stability, and an attractive investment environment could attract billions of dollars of capital from nationals and foreign investors.

In a chapter in a recent *Human Development Report* entitled "Still an Unequal World," the main message was

In no society today do women enjoy the same opportunities as men.

And the supporting messages:

This unequal status leaves considerable disparities between how much women contribute to human development and how little they share in its benefits.

A widespread pattern of inequality between women and men persists—in their access to education, health and nutrition, and even more in their participation in the economic and political spheres.

Women now share much more in the benefits of social services, both public and private—but continue to be denied equal opportunities for political and economic participation.

Women do not enjoy the same protection and rights as men in the laws of many countries.

Announced in the opening paragraph of that chapter, these messages drove the headings for the content that followed.

Here's the main message for a short policy brief on population projections from the Census Bureau:

As the U.S. population rises by 72 million over the next 30 years—to 335 million in 2025—more of us will live in the South and West, be elderly, and have Hispanic and Asian roots.

And the supporting messages, with their numerical detail:

The South and West will add 59 million residents by 2025— 82 percent of the projected growth to 2025—with more than

30 million people in just three states: California, Texas, and Florida.

Also by 2025, the population 65 and older will rise by 28 million people—39 percent of the projected growth—and bring to 27 the number of states where a fifth of their people will be elderly. Only Florida is close today.

The Hispanic and Asian populations will together gain 44 million people and constitute 24 percent of the total population in 2025, up from 14 percent today. California, Texas, and Florida will gain 20 million Hispanics.

Again, these four sentences were strung together—with bullets—to open the brief and, as you'll see in the next chapters, drive the headings for the content that followed.

3

USE YOUR SUPPORTING MESSAGES TO DEVELOP AN OUTLINE

THERE are many ways to break up your topic. For a short piece, look at your main message and see whether the topic lends itself to orderly division. For a long piece, try to discern the relations among the supporting messages to come up with your section headings. Will you move from the general to the particular? Will you divide a problem into its parts? Will you consider different things at different times? Will you group things or separate them? Your section headings should reflect your treatment of the topic.

Subsections are broken up in the same way as sections. If you have two or three sections and the piece is 15 to 20 pages long, you might want as many as four or five subsections in each section. But if you have many sections, you should have only a few subsections, if any, in each.

Your outline and, thus, your architecture will vary with your material, your audience, your constraints. The common structure of the typical academic research paper is *background, method, findings, implications,* and *conclusions,* headings that communicate no content. Compare those headings with *Rethinking the state—the world over,* which is beginning to communicate content. If you must use preordained section headings, try getting creative with your subsection headings, letting your messages drive them rather than the section headings. And if that's not possible, try writing an executive summary with headings driven by your message structure.

These messages:

As the U.S. population rises by 72 million over the next 30 years—to 335 million in 2025—more of us will live in the South and West, be elderly, and have Hispanic and Asian roots.

The South and West will add 59 million residents by 2025—82 percent of the projected growth to 2025—with more than 30 million people in just three states: California, Texas, and Florida.

Also by 2025, the population 65 and older will rise by 28 million people—39 percent of the projected growth—and bring to 27 the number of states where a fifth of their people will be elderly. Only Florida is close today.

The Hispanic and Asian populations will together gain 44 million people and constitute 24 percent of the total population in 2025, up from 14 percent today. California, Texas, and Florida will have 20 million Hispanics.

became the pillars of this outline:

Americans Are Getting Older, Warmer, More Diverse
Opening (no section heading)
    1. Different paths to growth
    2. 27 Floridas
    3. Big gains for Hispanics and Asians

Note how this outline (and eventual table of contents) communicates the essence of the report's content to readers:

Claiming the Future — Choosing Prosperity in the Middle East and North Africa

1. Disengagement from the changing global economy
   a. Missing out on globalization
   b. Domestic policies are ill suited to new global realities
2. Yesterday's achievements, today's predicament
   a. Achievements of the statist era were considerable
   b. Past successes were the outcome of easier times, not statist policies
   c. Why change has been slow
3. The promise of prosperity
   a. Some aspects of the international environment are favorable
   b. Many of the conditions in the Middle East and North Africa are favorable
   c. Jordan, Morocco, and Tunisia are beginning to reap the rewards of reform
4. From politics to economics
   a. Now is the time for action
   b. Choosing to be prosperous
   c. Politics in the service of economics

As does this:

The State in a Changing World

1. Rethinking the state — the world over
   a. The evolving role of the state
   b. Refocusing on the effectiveness of the state
2. Matching role to capability
   a. Securing the economic and social fundamentals
   b. Fostering markets: liberalization, regulation, and industrial policy
3. Reinvigorating institutional capability
   a. Building institutions for a capable public sector

    b. Restraining arbitrary state action and corruption
    c. Bringing the state closer to people
    d. Facilitating international collective action
  4. Removing obstacles to change
    a. The challenge of initiating and sustaining reform
    b. The agenda for change

4

DECIDE HOW LONG EACH SECTION WILL BE

AFTER you have developed an outline, decide how many paragraphs you will have in each section and subsection. Start with the number of pages you feel appropriate for the entire piece. Because double-spaced typescript usually has 2 to 3 paragraphs per page and single-spaced 4 to 5, multiply the number of pages by 2.5 for double-spaced typescript or 4 for single-spaced, the average number of paragraphs per page. The reason for doing this is that pages are merely units of display, while paragraphs are units of composition.

For the Census Bureau's policy brief on population projections to 2025, we came up with a maximum of 6 double-spaced pages and assigned them thus:

Americans Are Getting Older, Warmer, More Diverse

	No. double-spaced pages	No. paragraphs
Total	6	16
(Opening—no heading)	1	2
Different paths to growth	2	5
27 Floridas	1	3
Big gains for Hispanics and Asians	2	6

For the overview of the recent *World Development Report* on the state in a changing world, the estimated length was 30 pages. That meant about 75 paragraphs (2.5 × 30), which were assigned to the various sections and subsections in this way:

The Future of the State

	No. double-spaced pages	No. paragraphs
Total	30	75
Opening	2	5
Rethinking the state—the world over	2	5
A two-part strategy	2	3
Matching role to capability	7	16
The first job of states: getting the fundamentals right		7
Going beyond the basics: the state need not be the sole provider		6
Knowing the states limits		3
Reinvigorating state institutions	10	25
Effective rules and restraints		4
Subjecting the state to more competition		9
Bringing the state closer to people		9
Strategic options for reform		3
Beyond national borders: facilitating global action	3	10
Collective action		5
Embracing external competition		3
Promoting global collective action		2
Removing obstacles to state reform	4	11

When do reforms occur?   3
How can reform be sustained?   3
Good government is not a
    luxury—it is a vital necessity for
    development   5

5

CREATE A PARAGRAPH-BY-PARAGRAPH PLAN

YOU now know roughly the number of paragraphs you will have in each section. The next step is to assign a topic to each of those paragraphs. What you will end up with is a list of paragraph topics in the order they will appear in your report, interspersed among your section and subsection headings—in short, a paragraph-by-paragraph plan of places to gather your material. Don't worry about getting the list of paragraph topics right the first time. The first list will suggest other topics in different order. And as you begin to write, many of the topics will be divided or collapsed. But the more time you spend on this, the more solid the structure of your argument.

Paragraph-by-paragraph plans can be made at any stage of the writing process. I often prepare one for manuscripts that I edit—to get me quickly up to speed on content, structure, and balance. But it is most helpful to make one in the planning stage, after you've determined your messages and section headings, and then revise it when you have completed your first draft. The revised one will help you stay aware of changes in structure and the continuing relevance of your messages. Showing your paragraph plan to the people who will be reviewing your report—or to your fellow authors in a group project—is a good way to have them buy into what you're planning write. It also allows them to comment before you've invested a lot of time in writing.

Here is the paragraph-by-paragraph plan for the Census Bureau's policy brief:

Introduction (no heading)
¶1. Summary of messages

¶2. Quotation from analyst Paul Campbell: "Keep in mind that these are just projections . . ."

Different paths to growth
¶3. California, Texas, and Florida take different paths

¶4. California's losses through interstate migration

¶5. Texas's gains from all three contributors

¶6. Florida's small natural increase

¶7. Biggest interstate migration—New York

27 Floridas
¶8. 27 states will have one in five people elderly

¶9. 21 states will double their 65 and older population

¶10. Youth population—Alaska will have largest gains

Big gains for Hispanics and Asians
¶11. Hispanics and Asians and Pacific Islanders—61 percent of the growth

¶12. Big gains in California and the East

¶13. Growth in Black population in Georgia, Texas, Florida, Maryland, and Virginia

¶14. Growth in White population in Florida, Texas, Washington, North Carolina, and Georgia

¶15. Native American population rising

¶16. Campbell quotation: "What might seem unusual today will be usual tomorrow . . ."

6

MAKE A STRONG POINT ABOUT EACH OF YOUR PARAGRAPH TOPICS

WRITE the first topic of your paragraph-by-paragraph plan at the top of a sheet of paper (or at the top of a fresh page on your word processor), and make a strong point about it. If you have a general topic such as this:

Topic Partnerships of governments, businesses, and citizens

you might move to a strong point such as this:

Point When governments listen to businesses and citizens and work in partnership with them in deciding and implementing policy, they create programs that people will support.

Now do the same for all the other topics in your plan. You'll find for some that it's easy, and for others, impossible — and that will suggest refinements to your plan.

Here are some examples of moving from topic to point for the Census Bureau's brief on projections:

Topic California, Texas, and Florida take different paths

↓

Point California, Texas, and Florida will probably see the most growth but they will grow in very different ways.

Topic California's losses through interstate migration

↓

Point California will see big gains through natural increase and international migration but big losses through interstate migration.

Topic Texas's gains from all three contributors

↓

Point In Texas there will be a balance among all three contributors to its rising population.

Here's a set of topic-to-point conversions for the overview of the recent *World Development Report*:

Topic New ideas about the role of the state

↓

Point The world is changing and with it our ideas about the state's role in economic and social development.

Topic Expectations met, but not everywhere

↓

Point In a few countries things have indeed worked out more or less as the technocrats expected, but in many countries outcomes were very different.

Topic   Government getting bigger

↓

Point   Over the last century the size and scope of government have expanded enormously, particularly in the industrial countries.

Topic   Focus on state inspired by dramatic events

↓

Point   As in the 1940s, today's renewed focus on the state's role has been inspired by dramatic events in the global economy, which have fundamentally changed the environment in which states operate.

Topic   Clamor for more effective governance

↓

Point   The clamor for greater government effectiveness has reached crisis proportions in many developing countries where the state has failed to deliver even such fundamental public goods as roads, property rights, and basic health and education.

7

GATHER YOUR DETAILS, EXAMPLES, AND COMMENTS

ON each page, under each point—20 for a 20-paragraph report, 100 for a 100-paragraph report—begin noting your support—data, details, examples, and comments. It helps to spread all your pages out on a large table. I generally carry them around in a binder. That allows jotting down—and not losing—ideas that come to mind. It also allows working on one paragraph at a time.

The support for some of your points will fill some pages quickly, while others remain empty. If one point is short on detail and examples, you may need to compile more information by doing more research. If you can't support a point well, consider cutting it. And remember, an ounce of example is worth a ton of abstract generalization.

Here are examples from the Rockefeller Foundation's report:

Point The integrated model provides in-depth training in the skills required for a specific job and—just as important—places heavy emphasis on work habits.

Support Less intensive programs offer little to those with special disadvantages

> • Development of life skills
> • Stresses punctuality and attendance

Point   The integrated model provides literacy and numeracy training concurrently with job training.

Support   Only elements directly related to job included
> • Just-in-time remediation of basic skills speeds learning process
> • The closer the tie between job skills and basic literacy and numeracy training, the more willing trainees are to increase basic skills

Point   Another key feature of the integrated model is to have the education and employment program plugged directly into the requirements of industry—and to have industry plugged into the development of the program.

Support   When the demand and wages for a skill fall, it is phased out of the skill offerings
> • Technical instructors drawn from industry
> • Approach treats training as a business

Having all your material slotted into a paragraph-by-paragraph plan enables you to refine it *before* you've written a paragraph.

8

CONVERT YOUR RAW MATERIAL INTO DRAFT PARAGRAPHS

WITH the contents of each paragraph roughed out, the material of your paragraphs is now before you. Writing the perfect paragraph still won't be easy, but it should be much easier now that you have planned the order and content of each one.

Rough out your paragraphs by numbering your supporting elements—details, examples, and comments—in the order they might appear. Details that complement each other might be combined into one sentence. Paragraphs that are long and bristling with numbers may work better as a table or chart. Be especially careful to put dates or statistics in a logical order. Strike out unnecessary detail, and move elsewhere material that is not relevant to your point.

California will see big gains through natural increase and international migration but big losses through interstate migration.

- Projected increase of 17.7 million residents in the next 30 years
- California is the most populous state
- One in eight Americans live in California

- One in seven Americans will live in California by 2025
- The largest natural increase
- The largest net international migration
- The second largest inflow of interstate migrants
- The largest outflow of interstate migrants

The paragraph:

> With California's projected increase of 17.7 million residents in the next 30 years, one American in seven will live in California by 2025, up from one in eight today. For this most populous of states, everything happens in a big way: the largest natural increase, the largest net international migration, the second largest inflow of interstate migrants, and the largest outflow of interstate migrants.

A solid first draft.

The following sections contain a few paragraph models (drawn from Part Two) to help you convert your raw material into draft paragraphs.

LEAD WITH THE POINT AND SUPPORT IT

The most common way to develop a paragraph is to state the point in the first sentence and support it, in subsequent sentences, with evidence: details, examples, and comments. When you lead with the point, your reader can identify it immediately, and a skimmer can pick up your line of argument by reading the first sentence of each paragraph. This form of development is what most of us use for two-thirds of our writing. It becomes less effective when overused, and more when alternated with other ways of developing a point.

> *Over the past century, the human race has been affected by a slew of what demographers call "secular" trends. One such*

trend is an increase in average size. You have to stoop to get through the doorways of a Tudor cottage in England because its inhabitants were smaller than you are, not because they had a penchant for crouching. Another trend is in life expectancy. People are living longer. Life expectancy in Africa increased over the past 20 years from 46 to 53 years. Over the same period in Europe, where things were already pretty comfortable to begin with, life expectancy increased from 71 to 75 years. The global average was an increase from 58 to 65 years.

LEAD WITH THE POINT AND CONCLUDE WITH A COMMENT

Concluding a paragraph with a comment can inject a bit of your personality and, at times, humor. A comment can also put a paragraph in perspective, create a bridge to the next paragraph, or reinforce your point after presenting a series of facts.

> *Geography is not geology, but they can be interlinked in surprising ways.* Geographically, Sakhalin Island is part of the Russian Far East, though half of it was Japanese territory until 1945. Geographically, though, it is a northward extension of Japan and thus prone to the same sort of seismic ups and downs as the rest of that archipelago. Earthquakes are no respectors of political boundaries.

LEAD WITH THE POINT AND FOLLOW IT WITH A BULLETED LIST

A list of numerical facts, complicated details, or recommendations can be difficult for readers to lift off the page from a block of text. Breaking that block into bulleted items clarifies those elements, a style good for setting up a line of argument.

The ratio of global trade to GDP has been rising over the past decade, but it has been falling for 44 developing countries, with more than a billion people. *The least developed countries, with 10% of the world's people, have only 0.3% of world trade* — half their share of two decades ago.

The list goes on:

- More than half of all developing countries have been bypassed by foreign direct investment, two-thirds of which has gone to only eight developing countries.
- Real commodity prices in the 1990s were 45% lower than those in the 1980s — and 10% lower than the lowest level during the Great Depression, reached in 1932.
- The terms of trade for the least developed countries have declined a cumulative 50% over the past 25 years.
- Average tariffs on industry country imports from the least developed countries are 30% higher than the global average.
- Developing countries lose about $60 billion a year from agricultural subsidies and barriers to textile exports in industrial nations.

CONCLUDE WITH THE POINT AFTER INTRODUCING THE SUBJECT

Occasionally, put the point at the end of a paragraph to build suspense. One way to conclude with the point: introduce a subject, discuss it, then make a point about it at the end.

Imagine that a mad scientist went back to 1950 and offered to transport the median family to the wondrous world of the 1990s, and to place them at, say, the 25th percentile level. The 25th percentile of 1996 is a clear material improvement over the median of 1950. Would they accept his offer? Almost surely not—because in 1950 they were middle class, while in 1996 they would be poor, even if they lived better in material terms. *People don't just care about their absolute material level, they care about their level compared with others.*

START WITH A QUESTION AND ANSWER IT IMMEDIATELY

Asking a question in the first line of a paragraph grabs readers' attention and sets up your point. Using an immediate, direct answer to make your point demonstrates a firm stance, emphasized by the surety of a fragment.

So will squash eventually rival tennis as a spectator sport, and will Jansher Khan and Peter Marshall become as rich and famous as Pete Sampras and Andre Agassi? *Almost certainly not.* For all the gimmicks of a glasswalled court, a special white ball and more and better cameras, squash remains fearsomely difficult to televise. Not only does the ball move too fast but the camera lens foreshortens the action. Squash, therefore, is destined to remain a sport better played than watched. Given its propensity for what the tennis authorities term "audible obscenities", that may be just as well.

9

TAPE YOUR DRAFT ON A WALL TO APPLY THE FINISHING TOUCHES

A little-used but wildly effective technique is taping your entire draft report on a wall. That permits many things. One is to see more than a page at a time—indeed, to see all the pages at a time. Only by so doing can you assess overall structure and the balance of your sections and subsections. This also makes it easier to track your various levels of headings, switching sections to subsections and vice versa. And it makes it easier to revise your headings, injecting more punch, ensuring parallel treatment as appropriate.

A second virtue of taping your draft on a wall is that it puts the writer and reviewer side by side, dealing with the problems of a draft, rather than face to face, in the usually uncomfortable confrontation.

A third is that it allows you to make cuts quickly. If you need to cut a 50-page draft to 20 or 30 pages, it's the best technique. I use it for slash-and-burn editing, especially *stripping*—crossing out most sentences in a succession of paragraphs—lifting the points, and then stringing the points together to form new paragraphs.

REVIEW YOUR LINE OF ARGUMENT

To distinguish the levels of your headings, use a marker to circle all your A-level section headings and underline all your B-level subsection headings. Are there blocks of argument that would work better elsewhere? Look first at your sections, seeing whether you should move any of them. Next look at your subsections—and then at your paragraphs. Ask yourself whether your ideas flow in a logical and obvious way. If not, you may want to change some of your section and subsection headings to make the progression of your argument clearer.

SPOTLIGHT YOUR MESSAGES

The messages of a report or chapter are too often buried in the last 3 or 4 pages. Move them up front so that readers don't have to wait for them. Your readers should know your main message after reading only the first few paragraphs.

ADJUST LENGTH AND BALANCE

Think again about your target audience. How much do your readers really want, or need, to read? Look for duplication of information across sections, for long explanations of concepts that your readers may already know, and for tangents that side-track your argument. If you have a highly detailed or technical section, consider making it an appendix at the end of your report. If you cut or combine sections, you may need to adjust the balance of your report. Try to keep the sections roughly similar in length.

REFINE YOUR TITLE AND SECTION HEADINGS

You've been continually revising your title, now give it another test. Does it convey your message? For the example here, we moved from this title:

Growing the Economies of the Middle East and North Africa

to:

Claiming the Future: Choosing Prosperity in the Middle East and North Africa

After the title, take a look at headings. How could they better convey your messages? Headings engage your reader, so don't leave them empty.

A two-hour wall session with the lead authors of a World Bank policy research report on aid effectiveness began with this outline of headings:

Rethinking Aid

The new international environment
New thinking on development strategy
Aid and development
Aid, policy reform, and conditionality
Aid and public expenditures
Aid and the institutions for public services
Rethinking development agencies

Those became:

Assessing Aid: What Works, What Doesn't, and Why

New thinking on development strategy
Money matters in a good policy environment

Aid as the midwife of good policies
Money matters—in a good institutional environment
Aid as the midwife of good institutions
Moving aid from money to ideas

Far more informative.

TAKE A LAST LOOK

Before ripping your report off the wall, make sure that any
changes you made in the last few sections didn't displace
another element. Now you are ready to edit line by line to make
your report absolutely riveting. (See Parts Two and Three of this
book and *Edit Yourself*.) Last, do a spell-check and final leaf-
through to pick up incidental flaws that might unnecessarily distract your readers.

EXEMPLARY REPORTS: FROM START TO FINISH

From a policy brief for the U.S. Census Bureau

TOPIC, AUDIENCE, AND PURPOSE

What's the main topic?

State-by-state population changes to 2025

Who's going to read what you write?

Regular Census Brief distribution list of several thousand journalists, businesspeople, academics, and commerce colleagues

What's your purpose in writing?

To spotlight the marginal changes in population by region, by age group, by race/ethnic group—with state stories where interesting

How long should your report be?

6 double-spaced pages, or 15 paragraphs

How much time can you spend writing?

> Draft plan: 1/2 day (deadline: September 15)
> Draft brief: 5 days, 8 hours a day (deadline: September 28)
> (Printing in early October)

What's your working title?

> Americans Are Getting Warmer, Older, More Diverse

MESSAGES

What is the message you want to convey?

> As the U.S. population rises by 72 million over the next 30 years—to 335 million in 2025—more of us will live in the South and West, be elderly, and have Hispanic and Asian roots.

What are the supporting messages?

> • The South and West will add 59 million residents by 2025— 82 percent of the projected growth to 2025—with more than 30 million people in just three states: California, Texas, and Florida.
>
> • Also by 2025, the population 65 and older will rise by 28 million people—39 percent of the projected growth—and bring to 27 the number of states where a fifth of their people will be elderly. Only Florida is close today.
>
> • The Hispanic and Asian populations will together gain 44 million people and constitute 24 percent of the total population in 2025, up from 14 percent today. California, Texas, and Florida will gain 20 million Hispanics.

OUTLINE HEADINGS

Americans Are Getting Older, Warmer, More Diverse

	No. double-spaced pages	No. paragraphs
Total	6	16
Sections		
(Opening—no heading)	1	2
Different paths to growth	2	5
27 Floridas	1	3
Big gains for Hispanics and Asians	2	6

PARAGRAPH PLAN

Introduction (no heading)
¶1. Older, warmer, more diverse
¶2. Quotation from analyst Paul Campbell: "Keep in mind that these are just projections . . ."

Different paths to growth
¶3. California, Texas, and Florida take different paths
¶4. California's losses through interstate migration
¶5. Texas's gains from all three contributors
¶6. Florida's small natural increase
¶7. Biggest interstate migration—New York

27 Floridas
¶8. 27 states will have one in five people elderly
¶9. 21 states will double their 65 and older population
¶10. Youth population—Alaska will have largest gains

Big gains for Hispanics and Asians
¶11. Hispanics and Asians and Pacific Islanders—61 percent of the growth

¶12. Big gains in California and the East

¶13. Growth in Black population in Georgia, Texas, Florida, Maryland, and Virginia

¶14. Growth in White population in Florida, Texas, Washington, North Carolina, and Georgia

¶15. American Indian population rising

¶16. Campbell quotation: "What might seem unusual today will be usual tomorrow . . ."

SAMPLE PARAGRAPH CONTENTS

Paragraph topic:

California's losses through interstate migration

Make a strong point about the topic:

California will see big gains through natural increase and international migration but big losses through interstate migration.

List your supporting details, examples, and comments:

- Projected increase of 17.7 millions residents in the next 30 years
- California is the most populous state
- One in eight Americans lives in California
- One in seven will live in California by 2025
- The largest natural increase
- The largest net international migration
- The second largest inflow of interstate migrants
- The largest outflow of interstate migrants

Paragraph draft:

California's losses through interstate migration. With its projected increase of 17.7 million residents in the next 30 years, one American in seven will live in California by 2025, up from one in eight today. For this most populous of states, everything happens in a big way: the largest natural increase, the largest net international migration, the second largest inflow of interstate migrants, and the largest outflow of interstate migrants.

FIRST DRAFT

Getting Warmer, Older, More Diverse: State-by-State Population Changes to 2025

As the U.S. population rises by 72 million over the next 30 years—to 335 million in 2025—more of us will live in the South and West, be elderly, and have Hispanic and Asian roots.

- The South and West will add 59 million residents by 2025—82 percent of the projected growth to 2025—with more than 30 million people in just three states: California, Texas, and Florida.
- Also by 2025, the population 65 and older will rise by 28 million people—39 percent of the projected growth—and bring to 27 the number of states where a fifth of their people will be elderly. Only Florida is close today.
- The Hispanic and Asian populations will together gain 44 million people and constitute 24 percent of the total population in 2025, up from 14 percent today. California, Texas, and Florida will gain 20 million Hispanics.

Putting these numbers in perspective, Census Bureau analyst Paul Campbell said, "Keep in mind that these are just projections. I don't think we're wrong about the big trends, such as regional growth or the growth in the population 65 and older. But the projections do not drive reality. They come from projecting past trends into the future, and those trends can change — especially international migration, state-to-state movements, even births and deaths."

Different paths to growth

California, Texas, and Florida are expected to account for 45 percent of the nation's population growth from 1995 to 2025. But the main contributors to rising population — natural increase, interstate migration, and international migration — operate very differently in the three states.

California's losses through interstate migration. With its projected increase of 17.7 million residents in the next 30 years, one American in seven will live in California by 2025, up from one in eight today. For this most populous of states, everything happens in a big way: the largest natural increase, the largest net international migration, the second largest inflow of interstate migrants, and the largest outflow of interstate migrants.

Texas's gains from all three contributors. Distinguishing Texas's increase of 8.5 million is the balance among all three contributors to its rising population — with a large natural increase, high net interstate migration, and significant net international migration.

Florida's small natural increase. For Florida's increase of 6.5 million people from 1995 to 2025, the natural increase is low because of its already gray population. But it has the highest net interstate migration along with substantial net international migration.

The biggest interstate migration story is New York, which loses 13.1 million residents to other states and attracts only 8.0 million new residents, for a net loss of 5.1 million. By 2020 Florida will replace New York as the third most populous state.

27 Floridas

With baby boomers beginning to hit retirement age in 2010, 27 states will have one in five people elderly in 2025. And every state but Alaska and California will have 15 percent or more of their population 65 and older in 2025, up from a mere four states in 1995.

Twenty-one states will at least double their 65 and older population. Except for New Hampshire, all these states are in the South or West.

What about the other end of the age structure? Alaska will have the greatest proportion of its population under 20 years of age in 2025, followed by California, Utah, Texas, and New Mexico.

Big gains for Hispanics and Asians

Hispanics and Asians and Pacific Islanders, with 14 percent of today's population, will drive 61 percent of the growth — 44 percent from Hispanics and 17 percent from Asians.

California will add 12 million Hispanics to its population while Texas and Florida combined will add 8 million Hispanics. Forty-one percent of the nation's Asian population will live in California, with a jump from 3.6 million in 1995 to 9.1 million in 2025. But there will also be big gains in the East for Asians, with New York and New Jersey adding a combined 3.0 (or 1.6) million by 2025.

Florida and Texas are each expected to add about 1.9 million Blacks to their populations — and along with California, they will surpass New York as the states with the largest Black population. Most of the growth for Blacks will be in Georgia, Texas, Florida, Maryland, and Virginia.

And most of that for Whites will be in Florida, Texas, Washington, North Carolina, and Georgia.

The American Indian population is set to rise by nearly half, with the biggest gains in New Mexico, Oklahoma, and

Arizona. In 2025, about 46 percent of American Indians will reside in just five states—Oklahoma, Arizona, New Mexico, California, and Washington.

As Campbell concluded, "What might seem unusual today will be usual tomorrow, as our population continues to grow older, more diverse, more interested in living in the South and West."

EXEMPLARY REPORTS: FROM PLAN TO DRAFT

From the overview to the World Development Report 1997

HERE'S a look at the hierarchy of drafting, moving from topic → point → raw material → draft paragraph:

Topic   New ideas about the role of the state

↓

Point   The world is changing and with it our ideas about the state's role in economic and social development.

↓

Support   • Focus on state today similar to past
            • Changing role brought about by dramatic events
            • State saw itself as leader for change, too simplistic
            • Development was viewed as a largely technical challenge
            • Flexibility valued over checks and balances

↓

Draft   The world is changing and with it our ideas about the state's role in economic and social development. Today's intense focus on the state's role is reminiscent of an earlier era, when the world was emerging from the ravages of World War II, and much of the developing world was just gaining its independence. Then development seemed a more easily surmountable—and largely technical—challenge. State-led intervention emphasized market failures and accorded the state a central role in correcting them. But this worldview, as we all realize today, was too simplistic. Flexibility to implement policies devised by technocrats was accorded pride of place. Accountability through checks and balances was regarded as an encumbrance.

Topic   Expectations met, but not everywhere

↓

Point   In a few countries things have indeed worked out more or less as the technocrats expected, but in many countries outcomes were very different.

↓

Support   • Government schemes
• Private investors held back
• Rulers acted arbitrarily
• Corruption grew
• Development faltered

↓

Draft   In a few countries things have indeed worked out more or less as technocrats expected, but in many countries outcomes were very different. Governments embarked on fanciful schemes. Private investors, lacking confidence in public policies or in the steadfastness of leaders, held back. Powerful rulers acted arbitrarily. Corruption became endemic. Development faltered, and poverty endured.

Topic   Government getting bigger

↓

Point   Over the last century the size and scope of government have expanded enormously, particularly in the industrial countries.

↓

Support • Pre–World War II expansion answer to heavy toll taken by Depression
           • Postwar confidence caused people to ask for even more
           • Industrial countries expanded welfare states
           • Developing countries embraced state-dominated development plans
           • Size and reach of government ballooned
           • Rough statistic on state spending
           • Shift from quantitative to qualitative

↓

Draft   Over the last century the size and scope of government have expanded enormously, particularly in the industrial countries. The pre–World War II expansion was driven by, among other factors, the need to address the heavy toll on economic and social systems brought on by the Great Depression. The postwar confidence in government bred demands for it to do more. Industrial economies expanded the welfare state, and much of the developing world embraced state-dominated development strategies. The result was a tremendous expansion in the size and reach of government worldwide. State spending now constitutes almost half of total income in the established industrial countries, and around a quarter in developing countries. But this very increase in the state's influence has also shifted the emphasis from the quantitative to the qualitative.

Topic   Clamor for more effective governance

↓

Point   The clamor for greater government effectiveness has reached crisis proportions in many developing countries where the state has failed to deliver even such fundamental public goods as property rights, roads, and basic health and education.

Support   • Poor services and people won't pay taxes
• Example in Soviet Union, Eastern Europe
• Collapse of central planning has other problems
• Citizens deprived of basic public goods
• In some places the state crumbles entirely

↓

Draft   The clamor for greater government effectiveness has reached crisis proportions in many developing countries where the state has failed to deliver even such fundamental public goods as property rights, roads, and basic health and education. There a vicious circle has taken hold: people and businesses respond to deteriorating public services by avoiding taxation, which leads to further deterioration in services. In the former Soviet Union and Central and Eastern Europe it was the state's long-term failure to deliver on its promises that led, finally, to its overthrow. But the collapse of central planning has created problems of its own. In the resulting vacuum, citizens are sometimes deprived of basic public goods such as law and order. At the limit, as in Afghanistan, Liberia, and Somalia, the state has sometimes crumbled entirely, leaving individuals and international agencies trying desperately to pick up the pieces.

From the Rockefeller Foundation's report *Into the Working World*

Topic   Findings of possible gains

↓

Point   New findings from a Rockefeller Foundation study spotlight the possible gains from fully integrated programs of education and employment.

↓

Support • Findings useful to people working under the Family Support Act
• Focuses on relating basic skills to particular job
• Support for everyday services like child care

Draft   New findings from a Rockefeller Foundation study spotlight the possible gains from fully integrated programs of education and employment. The findings demand the attention of those developing programs of basic education and employment under the Family Support Act. The integrated model focuses employment training on a specific job, relates basic skills training to that job, and tries to meet the precise needs of the local labor market. The model also pulls together support services for handling such everyday problems as child care.

Topic   One site with good results

↓

Point   One of the four sites tested in the Minority Female Single Parent experiment—San Jose's Center for Employment Training—used (indeed, developed) this design with remarkable results.

↓

Support   • Integrated program yielded better jobs and higher wages
             • Statistics
             • Program worked well for low-income single mothers
             • More efficient than traditional programs

↓

Draft   One of the four sites tested in the Minority Female Single Parent experiment—San Jose's Center for Employment Training—used (indeed, developed) this design with remarkable results. When compared with other programs using more traditional designs, the integrated program yielded better jobs and higher wages for a higher proportion of participants. It led to a 27 percent increase in employment and 47 percent higher pay. The integrated program worked well for one of the most difficult groups to get into the work force—low-income single mothers. Moreover, it produced large increases in employment for an amount comparable to what traditional programs spend for similarly disadvantaged enrollees.

Topic   In-depth training for a job

↓

Point   The integrated model provides in-depth training in the skills required for a specific job

↓

Support   • Other programs fall short for those with substantial disadvantages
              • More extensive skills training helps disadvantaged obtain jobs

↓

Draft   The integrated model provides in-depth training in the skills required for a specific job. Less-intensive job-search and work-orientation programs help some people find work, but such programs offer little hope to those with substan-tial disadvantages, such as low-income single mothers. By contrast, more extensive skills training—in, say, word processing or metalworking—can help disadvantaged trainees obtain good jobs.

Topic   The program placed heavy emphasis on work habits.

↓

Point   Acquiring job skills is only half the training.

                            ↓

Support   • Other half of training focuses on developing life skills
               • Develop workers ready to pick up more skills
               • Punctuality and attendance

                            ↓

Draft   Acquiring job skills is only half the training. The other
               half focuses on the development of life skills, self-
               esteem, and a work ethic. The goal is not merely to
               produce a skilled word processor or machine tool op-
               erator. It is to develop a worker who is punctual, effi-
               cient, cooperative, and ready to pick up more skills.
               The integrated model stresses punctuality and atten-
               dance to impart the rhythm of industry. Trainees
               punch in—not at 8:00 am, but at 7:55 so that they can
               be at their station by 8:00.

Topic   Plugged into industry

                            ↓

Point   Another key feature of the integrated model is to have
               the education and employment program plugged di-
               rectly into the requirements of industry—and to have
               industry plugged into the development of the program.

                            ↓

Support   • Program developers work with industry personnel to
                 develop curricula
               • Training phased out when no demand, added
                 when new demands appear

- Instructors drawn from industry
- Treats training as a business

↓

Draft   Another key feature of the integrated model is to have the education and employment program plugged directly into the requirements of industry—and to have industry plugged into the development of the program. Program developers work closely with production supervisors, personnel man-agers, and equal opportunity officers to find precisely the skills required and to develop curricula that meet those requirements. When the demand and wages for a skill fall, it is phased out of the skill offerings. When new opportunities appear, they are added. Just as important, technical instructors are drawn from industry. With many years of experience, they know what is needed on the job—the knowledge, skills, and traits needed for success. The integrated approach thus treats training as a business, with the program tailored to community needs, changing market conditions, and the trainee's future work site.

Topic   Wraparound support services

↓

Point   Low-income people frequently have big problems and unstable lives, and sorting out day-to-day affairs can conflict with training, so support services are provided in the integrated model.

↓

Support   • Continuing support
             • Easy access
             • Child care
             • Avoid fragmenting trainees' days

                         ↓

Draft   Low-income people frequently have big problems and
             unstable lives, and sorting out day-to-day affairs can
             conflict with training. To avoid such conflict, the in-
             tegrated model provides continuing support for the in-
             dividual. It bolsters the training by providing easy
             access to support services that can systematically re-
             solve everyday problems. And for low-income mothers,
             the integrated model provides essential child care—at
             the training site or at a nearby child care center. The
             goal is to avoid fragmenting trainees' days by bouncing
             them from one agency to another. Instead, the inte-
             grated model tries to provide one-stop continuity for all
             the support services a person needs.

SOURCES

Benton Foundation, *The Learning Connection: Schools in the Information Age* (Washington D.C.: Benton Foundation, 1997), pp. ii–iii.

"Geo-political Earthquake," *The Economist* 335, no. 7917 (3 June 1995): 45.

Paul Krugman, "The CPI and the Rat Race," *Slate* (slate.com), 21 December 1996.

The Rockefeller Foundation, *Into the Working World* (New York: The Rockefeller Foundation, 1990), pp. 2–12.

The Survival of the Fittest," *The Economist* 337, no. 7937 (21 October 1995): 92.

UNDP (United Nations Development Programme), *Human Development Report 1995* (New York: Oxford University Press, 1995), pp. 1–29.

UNDP–World Bank, *Water and Sanitation Program Annual Report, July 1994–June 1995* (Washington, D.C.: World Bank, 1996), pp. 64–65.

"Unjammed," *The Economist* 347, no. 8069 (23 May 1998): 74.

U.S. Department of Commerce, Economics and Statistics Administration, Bureau of the Census, *Warmer, Older, More Diverse: State-by-State Population Changes to 2025*, census brief (Washington, D.C.: U.S. Census Bureau, U.S. Department of Commerce, December 1996), CENBR/96-1.

World Bank, *Adjustment in Africa: Reforms, Results, and the Road Ahead* (New York: Oxford University Press, 1994) pp. v–vi.

World Bank, *Claiming the Future: Choosing Prosperity in the Middle East and North Africa* (Washington, D.C.: World Bank, 1995), pp. 1–13.

World Bank, *World Development Report 1997* (New York: Oxford University Press, 1997), pp. v–15.